"Michael Higgin's *Jean Vanier: Log [...]* eloquent and moving meditation on [...] human in a 'throwaway' culture where competition, [...] greed, and inequality reign supreme. Vanier's work among the physically and intellectually vulnerable reveals the cost and joy of radical love. By emphasizing our common frailty and the openness and capacity of the disabled to allow Jesus to find repose in their hearts—he challenges us to enflesh tenderness in our own lives, become 'God's refuge' in a largely uncaring world. A book to be treasured and reread."

—James Clarke, poet, judge, author of *L'Arche Journal: A Family's Experience in Jean Vanier's Community*

"This is a brilliant exposition of an extraordinary man and the many influences that have shaped him and his prophetic vision. Higgins has entered deeply into Vanier's life story and presents it with fascinating detail. I have known Vanier and been involved with his L'Arche communities since the mid-sixties but every chapter of this beautiful book reveals to me new dimensions of both the man and his life work."

—Bill Clarke, SJ
Spiritual Director, Ignatius Jesuit Centre, Guelph, Ontario

"Since 1964, Jean Vanier and many friends, with and without intellectual disabilities, have lived in community together. These international communities of L'Arche, and Faith and Light, show that peace on earth and goodwill among all people is possible. Michael Higgins brings his characteristic enthusiasm and wide-ranging cultural interests to this personal interpretation of the life and legacy of Jean Vanier."

—Carolyn Whitney-Brown, PhD, editor of *Jean Vanier: Essential Writings*

People of God

Remarkable Lives, Heroes of Faith

People of God is a series of inspiring biographies for the general reader. Each volume offers a compelling and honest narrative of the life of an important twentieth- or twenty-first-century Catholic. Some living and some now deceased, each of these women and men has known challenges and weaknesses familiar to most of us but responded to them in ways that call us to our own forms of heroism. Each offers a credible and concrete witness of faith, hope, and love to people of our own day.

John XXIII	Massimo Faggioli
Oscar Romero	Kevin Clarke
Thomas Merton	Michael W. Higgins
Francis	Michael Collins
Flannery O'Connor	Angela O'Donnell
Martin Sheen	Rose Pacatte
Jean Vanier	Michael W. Higgins
Dorothy Day	Patrick Jordan
Luis Antonio Tagle	Cindy Wooden
Georges and Pauline Vanier	Mary Francis Coady
Joseph Bernardin	Steven P. Millies
Corita Kent	Rose Pacatte
Daniel Rudd	Gary B. Agee
Helen Prejean	Joyce Duriga
Paul VI	Michael Collins
Thea Bowman	Maurice J. Nutt

More titles to follow. . . .

Jean Vanier

Logician of the Heart

Michael W. Higgins

LITURGICAL PRESS
Collegeville, Minnesota

www.litpress.org

1	2	3	4	5	6	7	8	9

Library of Congress Control Number: 2015945305

ISBN 978-0-8146-3710-4   978-0-8146-3735-7 (ebook)

To Sue Mosteller of the Congregation of St. Joseph—
a friend and associate of Jean Vanier's
of several decades standing,
a sublime witness to the spirit and philosophy
of L'Arche,
and a personal friend and spiritual mentor to me.

Contents

Acknowledgments

It has been a privilege and a grace to write this book. I have known Jean Vanier for many years—we cooperated on a major event at St. Jerome's University and we have exchanged letters around our respective publications. In addition, I have written on Vanier and his work for *The Literary Review of Canada* and *Commonweal*.

Interviews for this book and related research are greatly dependent on the technical skill and searching intelligence of producer and editor Kevin Burns. The extensive quotations that appear throughout the text and lack citations are the result of these oral interviews.

Especially important as a resource was the fifth chapter of *Power and Peril: The Catholic Church at the Crossroads*, by Michael W. Higgins and Douglas R. Letson (Toronto: HarperCollins, 2002), and the fourth chapter of *Stalking the Holy: The Pursuit of Saint-Making*, by Michael W. Higgins (Toronto: Anansi, 2006).

I am indebted both to the creative forbearance of my partner and wife, Krystyna, whose own pressing publication deadlines never deflected attention from my own work and whose generosity of spirit and magnanimity is boundless, and to the patient endurance of my administrative assistant, Ami, who contributed immensely to providing the time and space for the research and writing.

Various figures associated with L'Arche and longtime friends of Vanier's—including Sue Mosteller, Nathan Ball, and Carolyn Whitney-Brown—were especially helpful. Don Morrison provided funding for a trip to Trosly and shared, with Eleanor Clitheroe-Bell and myself, in a several-hour discussion with Jean on his home turf. This is all grist for the writer's mill. I wish also to thank my daughter, Sarah, an MFA graduate student at the University of British Columbia, who read the manuscript with her customary care and prepared the index.

And finally, President John Petillo of Sacred Heart University has been an encouraging resource throughout this and other writing projects.

Introduction

Jean Vanier is one of the most honored men on the planet. Not that he cares. Honors are important, for sure, but they are not for him. The honors he has received, he has received for those with whom he lives, those who never receive honors and often never receive any recognition at all. They are the marginalized, the forgotten, the detritus of society. They are not the company of the honored.

But they are his company: preferred, embraced, loved—unconditionally.

In an interview in *The United Church Observer* in November 2013, Vanier spoke frankly about why we need people with disabilities: there is a mystery with these people with disabilities; they are the very presence of Jesus. For sure we can see their fragility, their weakness, and their pain, but at the same time we recognize their special place with God. In fact as we—sometimes reluctantly, sometimes fearfully—enter ever so tentatively into relationship with them, we discover that they *change* us.

Vanier recounted for the interviewer his encounter with Andrew, a man with whom he spent a year living in community. One day Andrew went to see a cardiologist, and when he returned home Vanier asked him what happened.

1

Andrew said that the doctor had looked into his heart. Vanier then asked what the doctor saw in his heart, and Andrew replied: "He saw Jesus, of course."

Vanier then asked what Jesus does in his heart, and his theologically astute interlocutor said that "Il se repose"— Jesus takes his rest/quietness there.

This is what the mystics say. It is what the gospels say: Jesus lives in our hearts. In fact, Vanier mused, the great spiritual writer Etty Hillesum, who was to perish in Auschwitz, made much the same point when she argued that though there was not much God can do for us in the encompassing darkness of the Reich, we can give God our hearts and be God's refuge in the world, a world that rejects the Divine.

Providing a place for God to rest is part of the vocation, the ministry, and the witness of people who are disabled. There is something very particular in their kindness, in their affection. For a year Vanier lived at La Forestière with the most severely disabled members of the L'Arche home in Trosly-Breuil, the foundation or motherhouse of the world-wide network of community homes that live under the sign of the Ark. At La Forestière he would give them baths, and in so doing he discovered that it was a great and liberating mystery to touch the bodies of those who couldn't communicate verbally. In fact it was unnecessary to do so; their very bodies proclaimed "love me." Such a communication arose naturally from the very depths of who they are—they *are* their bodies, broken, ruptured, fragile, incomplete. But theirs are wrapped in love.

Their bodies are tender, and there is something deeply significant in that. Vanier remembers that at one point he asked their community psychiatrist what it means to be a pure human person, and he responded unhesitatingly: "tenderness."

It is tenderness that reveals our ability to speak with great respect of others and in a way that allows us to give security to them without actually possessing them. The tenderness of the disabled heals us, breaks us free from what Thomas Merton, quoting Albert Camus, calls the "plague of cerebration." For Vanier the intellectualizing of the faith by the church obscures the greater truth, a truth that is enfleshed and not conceptualized, the truth that allows the other, Jesus, Andrew, the unnamed and ignored, to rest in our hearts.

This is the essence of the teachings of Jesus. It is the principle, ethos, substratum, very life, and meaning of L'Arche itself: Jesus lives in our hearts as we live in his.

The L'Arche message is the text of the person of Jesus, his radicality. When we hold a meal it is not the familiar we should invite—the friends, the wealthy, and the affluent. Rather, it should be those who are poor, lame, blind, and disabled. This is not the doctrine of Nietzsche.

The tribe can crush the spirit; we need to break out of our secure orbit; we need to risk.

The people who are disabled are our reward.

And they remind us of the deeper truths, the truths that sustain us as a culture, humanize and ennoble us. This is never more imperative—this awareness, this memory—than now, when we are besotted with the allure of security, wealth, and access to chemicals and treatments that can prolong our escape from mortality. Those who are intellectually and physically challenged have no time for illusions; they force us to confront the *reality*, not the false dreamscape of humanness. They are the true sentinels of our larger hope.

In a time when the "throwaway culture" so vigorously condemned by Pope Francis still holds sway, and in a time when economic disparity has never been so wide, dangerously wide, the witness and teachings of Jean Vanier have never been so necessary.

Nobel Laureate Paul Krugman, a Harvard economics professor and *New York Times* columnist, does not tire in warning us that the wielders of power, the plutocrats and their compliant subordinates in industry and the capital exchanges, are not inclined to rethink the global geography, not disposed to redistribute wealth, not eager to embrace a different model of wealth generation itself. Fear and greed work in tandem to ensure the preservation of the status quo.

Krugman's spirited criticism of US monetary policy and the injustices perpetuated by the priests of Wall Street is grounded in a foundational moral insight: people are more than economic agents, buyers and sellers, and their deeper needs for community, a decent living, and a feeling of human solidarity are being ruthlessly undercut by a political and fiduciary regime hostile to fundamental structural change.

In sharp contrast to Krugman and his relentless critique is the editor of Britain's *The Spectator*, Fraser Nelson, who boldly declares that the 1 percent are worth their pay, that likely they will pull even further away from the other 99 percent, and that in the end, their unchecked capacity to create wealth will work to the advantage of the rest of us. Hence, the English prime minister best move cautiously in taxing them unreasonably and concentrate instead on improving the lot of the poor.

What is true, Fraser argues, of the United Kingdom and the United States is no less true of other sovereign jurisdictions—if less egregious in their income disparity—that the best way forward is a *reakpolitik* that leaves undisturbed the entrepreneurial instinct. This is preferable to the fanciful notion that a just society can be created on the backs of the 1 percent.

Fraser's Social Darwinism stands in sharp contrast with Krugman's classical morality, and their debate is joined by countless others in the halls of academe, the corridors of parliament and congress, and in the editorial rooms of the media industry, while the seeds of dissolution mature in the dark.

In the light stands the public, a humble and eloquent testament of an alternative strategy to the crass realism of a Nelson Fraser and an endorsement of an economics with a human face that you find in Krugman's impassioned thinking—and that light is Jean Vanier and his intentional communities. Vanier is not an economist, any more than Pope Francis. He does not issue periodic jeremiads, pronounce with oracular majesty from a distance, nor proffer solutions to complex politico-economic issues. What he does, like Jorge Mario Bergoglio, is offer a palpable alternative to being human whereby the homeless garner as much attention and sympathy as a dysfunctional celebrity or financial climber.

A moving and effective communication of Vanier's vision can be found in a correspondence conducted in the pages of Canada's national newspaper, *The Globe and Mail*, commencing on September 12, 2008, and concluding on January 2, 2010. The correspondents were Vanier himself and Ian Brown, an award-winning features writer and author, whose book *The Boy in the Moon: A Father's Search for His Disabled Son* had underscored with painful eloquence the quest of a parent to find meaning in the seemingly arbitrary and meaningless suffering of a severely disabled son.

Throughout their correspondence they spoke with sometimes searing honesty about their doubts, struggles, uncertainties, dreams, and hopes. And they did it in the pages of the country's leading paper of record and not in a religious journal of limited range and identifiable market. This was risky stuff—baring your soul for public consumption—particularly if one of the interlocutors was in no conventional way an orthodox believer or churchgoer.

But the risk was worth it, and at the heart of the correspondence the reader can see the burgeoning of a new and substantial friendship—borne in honesty, openness, and shared pain.

Brown, the father of Walker, the "boy in the moon" who was born with a rare genetic syndrome called cardio-facio-cutaneous syndrome, makes the trek to Trosly in April of 2008. He spends some time living in one of the L'Arche homes, La Semance, and develops an abiding affection with the residents. A few months after returning to Canada, Brown writes a lead-feature profile of his trip to Trosly and his encounter with Vanier.

Throughout his feature article on Vanier and the subsequent correspondence, there is a no-holds-barred dimension to their conversation. There is honesty and forthrightness in what they reveal about themselves and in what they say to each other. This isn't just a case for an apologia or a conventional profile; both men are on a quest for meaning and understanding.

Brown asks Vanier outright if he is afraid of dying, and he responds that he is not frightened of death but that he is of anguish. Vanier defines anguish to include fear and regret over not living the kind of life one is called to live. Like Adam in the Garden of Eden fearful of his nakedness we, too, are fearful of our nakedness, our mortality, and our incapacity to control our own lives. We are all vulnerable and we hate that; we can sign on for all the insurance we want but we are moving inexorably toward death.

Brown then segues to prayer; he notes that Walker, his son who is disabled, shares a language with him that consists of clicking his tongue. Walker is unable to speak and struggles to find a way to communicate. That clicking seems to Brown a form of prayer. Vanier responds unequivocally that it *is* praying because praying is not doing, it's clicking, it's compassion, thankfulness and peacefulness, gratitude and communion. "Prayer, then," Brown surmises, "is a way of reminding ourselves . . . ," and Vanier completes his thought with "to be who we are."

Amazed by the vitality, resourcefulness, and high purpose of L'Arche, Brown pries out of Vanier a reflection around the genesis, meaning, and evolution of L'Arche that constitutes an essential definition. In other words, Vanier condenses a book to a few paragraphs, edits exquisitely a life project in a conversation.

Vanier makes it clear that he did not begin L'Arche because he wanted to help some unfortunate people who were incarcerated in dismal and violent institutions, as worthy as that may be. He founded L'Arche because it was part of his larger yearning for peace. During the civil rights struggles in the United States in the 1960s—even earlier in the 50s—Vanier marveled at Martin Luther King's heroic struggle to establish the truth that all women and men have a right to be free, that each is a child of God. So, too, at L'Arche: a community that witnesses to the beauty and value of each person, irrespective of culture, race, nationality, creed, abilities, or disabilities.

People with disabilities, in particular, often lack a community that can bring them life. Human beings are not made to be alone. It is not what the Creator intended. Loneliness often begets hyperactivity because we need to compensate, and so we develop dependencies that are unhealthy, we become addicted, and we become frightfully competitive. And all this works against what we are meant to be: rooted in a place, bonded with others, supporting the weak, and comforting the strong.

In a competitive culture, individual success is privileged; those who are weak or disabled are seen at best as losers or a nuisance, and are quickly put aside, and in some cases eliminated.

Vanier never makes light of the struggles working with people who are disabled; he refuses to minimize their demands and in the process distinguishes between a religion that nurtures and one that constricts. He tells Brown that a closed religion accentuates rubrics, doctrines, and polity because they provide a form of security, whereas an open religion accentuates love for people that implies a great deal of risk and vulnerability. In other words: little in the way of security.

An open religion, in contrast to one that is closed, places great emphasis on freedom and bonding; there can be no false security built on a fabricated community. Everyone must be *real*. To that end, those who work and live in a L'Arche community must find the right balance between freedom and bonding, between individual needs and dreams and the imperatives of living together. That balance or harmony between what he terms competence and spirituality, Vanier argues, is something every L'Arche member, no matter novice or veteran, must always struggle with. It is a constant of genuine community living.

At the end of the Brown/Vanier correspondence, Vanier ruminates on the meaning of his life; he is now in his 80s, worries about what will happen to those with whom he lives once he has gone, and reflects on his loneliness following the death of Barbara, his secretary for four decades. He recounts her passing with simple eloquence and deep feeling.

He speaks of her fidelity, the fact that she was with him twenty-four hours a day and knew everything that he did and was called to be. He held her hand as she lay dying, as little by little her breath became slower and slower, agonizingly intermittent, until her breathing stopped. She slipped behind the veil of our mortality. He quotes Rabindranath Tagore when he says that death is not the lamp that goes out but the coming of dawn.

Vanier had hoped that Barbara would communicate with him, by dreams for instance. But there has been only silence, and all he can do is trust that she has forgiven him for all the many times when he did not sufficiently recognize the inestimable gift of herself.

While thinking of Barbara, Vanier does an autobiographical and metaphysical riff on the importance of L'Arche in itself and its impact on him. He remarks that he had no plan to cofound L'Arche, that he met people who were influential in forming his growth, people with disabilities that quickened his heart. They also revealed the shadow side of his personality—his anguish, anger, and fears.

But most importantly they opened him to his fragility, which in turn spurred him to form community, to be together in peace and friendship with others, those who are frail, dependent, and wounded.

For this to flourish there must be trust, which Vanier defines as the center and cornerstone of his life. In trust he comes to accept life and to foster it in others; in trust his life is born and reborn each day.

Throughout his correspondence with Ian Brown, Vanier spoke from the heart to the heart; he did so in the public arena, he displayed his own vulnerabilities, and he affirmed others in their aching into meaning.

Vintage Vanier!

CHAPTER ONE

The Vaniers

If there were an aristocracy in Canada, the Vanier family would be prominent on the list. Jean Vanier's parents were iconic figures during their tenure as a diplomatic duo and later as a vice-regal couple. Georges and Pauline Vanier have even been brought up as candidates for beatification with Monsignor Roger Quesnel of the Archdiocese of Ottawa, who is charged with the task of opening the investigation or preparatory phase prior to a formal introduction of the cause.

Pauline Vanier came from a family of estimable Quebec pedigree. Her mother, Thérèse de Salaberry Archer, was a profoundly pious woman who shared a spiritual director, the Jesuit Almire Pichon, with the Carmelite French mystic St. Thérèse de Lisieux, known to millions as the Little Flower. Her father was a Superior Court of Quebec justice.

Georges Vanier came from a prosperous business family that could trace its roots to the seventeenth century in New France. He studied law at Laval University, was instrumental in helping to organize the legendary Royal 22nd Regiment or "Van Doos," and returned from WWI a decorated officer sans one leg lost in battle.

Married in 1921 the Vaniers would soon be thrust into the demanding and hectic world of international diplomacy. Georges was appointed the first Canadian aide-de-camp to the new governor general Sir Julian Byng, the British war hero known as Lord Byng of Vimy, and was dispatched to spend two years at the prestigious Staff College for officers in Camberley in England. By the end of the decade he would find himself appointed Canada's representative on the League of Nations Permanent Advisory Commission for Naval, Military, and Air Questions and would be relocated to Geneva.

And it would be in this Swiss city where Jean was born on September 10, 1928. Biographer Mary Frances Coady records the unfolding drama of his birth in *Georges and Pauline Vanier: Portrait of a Couple* (2011). She writes that Pauline's labor pains came on so rapidly that there was little time to get the couple to the hospital by taxi. The physician arrived after the birth, and with a bit of native theatricality, Jean Francois Antoine was born. The time was less than auspicious for his father as he was to attend a Canadian delegation dinner, but Georges had no doubt where his priorities lay. With a typical sensitivity to the needs of others, he christened Jean "Jock," as the family's Scot nannies found the soft *J* difficult to pronounce.

Jock was the fourth of five children: Thérèse, Georges (Byngsie), and Bernard preceded him, and Michel followed. Jean/Jock's arrival in some key ways compounded the difficulties Pauline faced adjusting to the mounting demands of a diplomat's wife and young mother. In seven years of marriage there were five pregnancies, four births, five household moves, as well as dealing with the aftershocks of surviving a fire that destroyed their rented holiday house at Pointe-in-Pic, north of Quebec City. In addition, Pauline's emotional disposition, colored by a heightened religious sensitivity and periodic bouts of depression, although in great measure the source of her success as an extrovert "working" the social room and facilitating conversation as a host, stood in stark contrast to her accumulating anxiety and exhaustion on the domestic scene.

As a consequence, one of the nannies, Nancy Thompson, in effect became Jean's mother. Ironically, although Jean's arrival was heralded by his aunt Frances Vanier as a wonderful omen for peace, being born at the seat of the League of Nations, he did not appear to bring a great deal of peace to his emotionally overwhelmed mother. He was however only one of a series of causes for her depletion of energy, and it should be noted that their relationship over the years was actually marked by a special closeness, empathy, and spiritual understanding. But in 1928, it was different. In fact, at one point as biographer Mary Frances Coady records, Jock, the child most deeply affected by his mother's absence, was heard screaming at her, "I hate you! I am going to kill you."

Pauline's emotional health continued to decline. Georges was chosen as one of Canada's delegates to a naval conference to be held in London in 1930, and Pauline accompanied him as a secretary and host. In part, he was keen on giving her some respite, some space from the demands of Geneva and the growing family. But she would have a collapse and enter a convalescent home with the not uncommon diagnosis of the period: neurasthenia.

Shortly after Georges became the First Secretary to the Canadian High Commissioner in London, England became their home. Byngsie, Bernard, and Jock were enrolled in

St. John's, a Jesuit preparatory school for the upper-level Beaumont, also Jesuit in inspiration and instruction. Prior to admission, Bernard was judged by his previous school, Egerton, to be capable of making excellent progress and had demonstrated improved prowess with a cricket bat. Jock, by contrast, was judged a slow starter, somewhat inarticulate, full of undisciplined energy, disheveled and inattentive, restless and erratic. Not the best recommendation.

But life at St. John's wouldn't be forever. With war pending, Georges was promoted to be his country's ambassador to France, and the family moved to Paris. They withstood the early months of the war, but once Belgium and Holland fell, the safety of the family in France was imperiled. They began their escape. Jean himself recalls that in May and June of 1940 he was only eleven years old and a refugee in flight with his family, that they made it to the north of France where they were placed on a British destroyer and then put on a cargo ship that brought them to safety in England. But even that was to prove difficult. After several days at sea they arrived at Falmouth but couldn't dock because of mines in the port, so they were rerouted to Wales and arrived in the capital in time for the blitzkrieg.

This experience of the hell and chaos that is war was followed quickly by the family's endangered transatlantic crossing as they headed back to Canada in 1941. Jean remembers listening to an announcement on a Nazi English-language radio network that the ship they were on had been sunk. Rather than being anxious or fearful over this intelligence, Vanier recollects that he was thrilled to be part of a great adventure. After all, he was eleven years old.

Two years later Jean would approach his father with his plan to recross the Atlantic, head for England through U-boat infested waters, and join the Royal Naval College.

Rather than just dismissing the request as an example of an adolescent's romantic heroism, an offer too absurd to be taken seriously, Georges's considered, wise, and respectful response would leave a mark on his son's formation that was nothing less than transformational.

Jean recounts with minute accuracy the charged emotion and lasting impact of the conversation. His father asked him to explain why, at the age of thirteen and in the midst of a war, he really wanted to join the navy. When Jean told him his reasons, his father said that he trusted him and that if that is what he *wanted* to do then that is what he *must* do. Upon later reflection as a maturing adult, Jean reflected on that time as one of the truly healing moments of his life because he realized that his father, whom he loved and respected, trusted him, and in so doing allowed him to trust himself. Had Georges dismissed Jean's request as premature, if not silly, urging him to wait a few more years before applying to the Royal Navy, Jean would have accepted that as reasonable, if not disappointing. He remembers that at the time he was not especially rebellious; in fact, he was fragile. And if his father had been disinclined to take him seriously, Jean believes that he would have lost trust in his own "deep intuition."

This deep intuition came from a "holy part of my being . . . the sanctuary of my being," says Jean, and as a consequence, his father's response freed him to trust his own desires. As Jean understood it, his father was saying to him that he trusts his intuition, his desire, because it originates in God. His father's considered reaction to his request underlined for Jean what later would be an operating principle in his life and ministry: we must listen to the young because they have in them the light of God, and they will never be able to trust themselves unless someone trusts them first.

And so began the next phase in his life, a phase that would start with a farewell to his parents, a journey to England— fraught with peril—and enrollment in the navy college at Dartmouth. His adolescent years would be spent not in a prestigious grammar school preparing him for Oxbridge, but in a war college that would be bombed at the start of his second term (he and his fellow students were relocated for the duration of their studies), moving inexorably toward graduation and then assignment to the war theater. Except, by the time he finished his training, the war was over.

Still, the war directly touched him. Following the liberation of Paris in August 1944, Jean accompanied Pauline, who was working with the Canadian Red Cross (she had traveled to the "city of lights" when her husband took up his duties—the first accredited ambassador to do so after the flight of the Nazis) to the Gare d'Orsay. There he witnessed the tragic parade of destitute and broken victims: the survivors of Dachau, Buchenwald, Ravensbrook, and so forth, decamping from their trains, skeletons in striped blue and white uniforms, the badge of humiliation and damnation.

He recalls with a sad vividness the searing impression made on them both by the survivors' suffering and anguish. He could see now, as with the survivors of Hiroshima, the devastating capacity for self-destruction that lay within humanity's reach. He was not there to liberate the camps; he didn't taste firsthand the despair of Auschwitz, the madness of Treblinka, the morally inverted world of Terezin; but he did see the hopelessness and spiritual fragility of the survivors. Like all such memories, they would prove indelible.

Launched on his post-war career with the Royal Navy, he would in time transfer to the Canadian Navy. In this new role he traveled on board the HMCS *Magnificent* to Cuba, engaged in exercises with the United States Navy. While his

fellow officers amused themselves in the haunts and in the
company that appeal to seamen when on leave, Vanier spent
his time exploring local churches. And as many in his generation did, he devoured the phenomenally successful *The
Seven Storey Mountain*, the autobiography of Thomas Merton, the Cambridge- and Columbia-educated convert to
Catholicism who had become a global celebrity as a Trappist
monk in Gethsemani, Kentucky.

This is not surprising. There was a reawakening of religious fervor following the war, with many of the veterans
returning from the carnage of the European and Asian
battlegrounds hungering for direction in their lives. They
hungered for meaning in the new wasteland.

The Seven Storey Mountain offered a new vision; it offered a life of regulated prayer, ordered activity, genuine
community, and viable hope to a lost generation. That generation was Jean Vanier's. He came to maturity during the
war, and although only a teenager when he set off for England and Dartmouth, he experienced its immediacy, its
chaos, its destructiveness, and its lethality.

Merton would naturally appeal to a young man poised
to discover his path to God, keen on finding his way. Jean
was so engaged by his reading of Merton's autobiography
that he visited Friendship House in Harlem to taste something of the community *for* and *of* the poor embodied in
the vision of Catherine de Hueck. Catherine was a Russian
noble and now a resident in New York City, a convert to
Catholicism and alive to the gifts of poverty and humility,
the demands of social justice, and the imperative of racial
harmony.

Increasingly restless of spirit, Vanier began to think seriously of a shift in direction. He reasoned that when he was
in the navy he was accustomed to giving orders and that

that was second nature to him. He was well trained in the arts of ambition and success; he knew how to compete. But he was persuaded that in the process, community and communion suffered. The "I" triumphed at the expense of the "we."

In 1950, following a thirty-day Ignatian retreat—with the opportunity for deep discernment that it provided—Vanier resigned his commission in the navy. He was now ready for something new. But what?

CHAPTER TWO

Père Thomas
and Spiritual Friendship

Pauline Vanier intervened in the life of her son at a critical moment. Aware that this former navy officer was now adrift, she introduced him to a man who would prove a critical spiritual mentor for his life and vocation: Thomas Phillippe, a friar of the Order of Preachers or Dominicans.

Père Thomas was Pauline's spiritual director and a man of daunting spiritual gifts and quiet charisma. Like many of the distinguished French Dominican thinkers of his day, he was a Thomist, but more inclined by temperament and intellectual conviction to a conservative reading of the texts. He was not identified with the New Theologians, gathered around the Dominican Priory and House of Studies known as the Saulchoir and also situated at the Institut Catholique, theologians and philosophers increasingly seen as suspect by the Roman authorities. Because of the ferment of ideas at the Saulchoir and Rome's mounting disquiet, Phillippe was delegated to remove the eminent Dominican thinker, Marie-Dominique Chenu, which only magnified the distrust of others in his community who saw him as Rome's police officer. Tensions were magnified, and by 1947, the year he met Vanier, he finished his term as Master of Studies and retired from the fray. He would now turn his attention to what really fired his spirit: the mystical.

Père Thomas was determined to help people discover mysticism, not narrowly in a humanistic sense, but deeply embedded in an orthodox theology. To that end he founded Eau Vive, a small community in close proximity to the Saulchoir, where students, and not necessarily those intending to become Dominicans, could study philosophy and theology in the context of Christian living.

In Eau Vive, Père Thomas's "school of wisdom," Vanier recognized the Dominican's postwar vision: doing the "international work of the heart." His commitment to *doing* theology and philosophy in a community of prayer and love attracted Vanier, who would join the community in the fall of 1950. The catalyst for that decision was his meeting with Père Thomas. Vanier would recall years later that it was clear he needed "a master, a teacher, a spiritual father." He likened his response to Père Thomas to Jesus' summons to two disciples to leave John the Baptist and follow him, to come and see where he dwelled. The meeting with the mystical French friar was that transformative and foundational; Vanier followed and he dwelled.

Many years later Vanier would describe his first meeting with Père Thomas as one of the two great moments of truly liberating love. The other was his realizing that he had his father's trust at the age of thirteen, a trust that emancipated him.

Shortly after joining the community at Eau Vive, Vanier accompanied the founder to Rome for Pope Pius XII's formal proclamation of the dogma of the assumption of the Blessed Virgin Mary. The Mother of God played a central role in Père Thomas's mysticism, and this formal declaration of doctrine had enormous appeal to him. Vanier, in turn, saw significance in the fact that his "second conversion"—recognizing that a career defined by competition and advancement distracts from being a "maker" of community—occurred in the year of the assumption. In fact, he referred to himself as "child of the assumption."

For Père Thomas, functioning as Vanier's spiritual master was not a form of paternalism, control, or cultish manipulation. Quite the contrary. What it did was open Vanier to possibilities, vulnerabilities, and self-knowledge. He came to see that Christians had lost faith in the essential truths of the New Testament. In addition, modern Catholics had forgotten that all is love; that Jesus is *really* the Way, the Truth, and the Life; and that the cross is love and Jesus actually perished from an excess of love.

What happened to Chenu would now happen to Phillippe. Because of the understanding in both Dominican and curial circles that his theology of Mary was unorthodox and dangerously "mystical," subject to scrutiny by his superiors, he was removed from his position at Eau Vive and summoned to Rome in 1952. Vanier drove him to the Eternal City and would, although not without deep hesitation and subsequent political and canonical squabbling, succeed him as director of Eau Vive until his own summary removal by the Holy Office of the Inquisition in 1956.

In her biography of Vanier, *The Miracle, The Message, The Story: Jean Vanier and L'Arche*, Kathryn Spink highlights Vanier's indebtedness to Père Thomas's way of doing theology that has lasted to the present day with his own imaginative and poetic readings of the Gospel of John:

> Père Thomas's theology gave him strong and solid principles to the extent that he did not really seek anywhere else. They also gave him a freedom to think for himself so

that in later life, when concentrating on the gospels or theology he did not feel obliged, as others might, to quote other sources or authorities, but rather had a strong sense of the synthesis of his own knowledge and experience: "If people find that I am very free in my intellectual life," he was to write many years later, "even in my interpretation of the Gospel of St. John and in my development of an anthropology which is bound to human and spiritual reality, it was because I was moulded by the thinking and methods of Père Thomas."[1]

Relieved of his responsibilities at Eau Vive, Vanier pondered the call to priesthood. It was something he had considered for some time in large part at the behest of Thomas and his brother Marie-Dominique, also a Dominican, a move that would ensure a priestly oversight of Eau Vive. The plan seemed simple enough: Vanier would study philosophy and theology in Paris, return to Canada to finish his final year at the Grande Seminaire in Quebec City, where he would be ordained for the Archdiocese of Quebec, return to France on secondment as the director of Eau Vive, and serve as well as chaplain to the Canadian students studying in Paris. But this plan was now in tatters.

With Thomas in Rome and shorn of his duties as director of Eau Vive, Vanier was unsure where his future lay. Time for a lengthy discernment. He found the place he needed at the Trappist Abbey of Nôtre Dame de Bellefontaine, and he spent a year there following the monastic *horarium*, praying and working with his hands, reading, and trying to understand and make sense of God's will for him.

At the end of his time in Bellefontaine, he had decided on two things: he would not pursue studies for the priesthood in Quebec, and he would seek out counsel from Père Thomas, who was after all his spiritual director.

Increasingly, Vanier became aware of the liberating truth that he was being called to witness to the gospels *outside* the traditional ecclesiastical structures, that he was being called to trust his intuition, his conscience, the "aboriginal Vicar of Christ" as Newman would argue, to remember what it meant to him to know that his father trusted him completely.[2]

To that end, but still unsure where precisely his vocational direction lay, Vanier pursued doctoral studies at the Institut Catholique concentrating his dissertation on Aristotle, whose thinking especially appealed to him. In many ways it was the epistemological and metaphysical realism of Aristotle that commanded his respect. In that, like much else, Vanier was a Thomist, like his Dominican mentors.

Vanier contrasted Plato's emphasis on the interior experience with Aristotle's preference for the external experience. He conceded that authentic Christianity is about a "harmonization" of the two perspectives, but that from a strictly philosophical point of view Aristotle's love of the tangible, the tactile, the senses, the *real* as opposed to the *ideal,* speaks to both his mind and his heart.

Vanier's dissertation on Aristotle was on his notion of happiness. It was published decades after the defense with undoubted amendments and adjustments occasioned by his evolving maturity as a man and as a thinker. *Made for Happiness: Discovering the Meaning of Life with Aristotle* speaks to Vanier's openness to Aristotle as both a philosophical and theological source for a renewed Christianity. Like Thomas Aquinas, Vanier has no difficulty probing the insights and revelations found in the work of the Philosopher.

Vanier saw in Aristotle one of the great witnesses to the human quest for happiness. Aristotle was grounded in the real and never took the route of the ideologue. He was fearless in his quest to identify the ethics of happiness and to do so in a way that privileged personal experience. He dispensed with issuing moral nostrums and dismissed any coercive means that compelled people to be just and to seek the truth. The foundations of an ethical life lie in our deepest desires. It is not so much what we ought to do—the imperatives that govern our behavior from the outside. Rather, the essential question to ask is what we truly desire. We must explore the deepest recesses of our heart in order to determine what it is that will bring us to ultimate fulfillment. Aristotle understood that a meaningful and fecund ethics has to be based on our *desire* for human happiness and not on some *idea* of human happiness.

It was because of his research into Aristotelian ethics that Vanier came to realize that both psychology and spirituality have key roles to play in the making of an ethical person. Psychology helps us to understand the nature of human behavior and to appreciate those neuroses and psychoses that work against human integration and harmony. Spirituality cleanses, deepens, and sustains our motivations for the true, the good, and the beautiful. Ethics itself enables us to better comprehend what is a truly human act, an act that brings us happiness as well as helps us to better grasp what our freedom is ever summoning us to do, to be. Being human in Aristotle's eyes involved maturity of judgment and not deference to laws; it meant becoming fully accomplished not only for our own individual sake but for the composite of humanity as a whole. The perfect human activity, then, the activity that leads us to happiness, includes seeking the truth in all that we do, spurning the false comfort of lies and illusions, always acting justly, and transcending oneself in order to act altruistically and unstintingly for the betterment of others and society.

We have models we can look to, as Vanier noted in *Made for Happiness: Discovering the Meaning of Life with Aristotle*:

> Aristotle in fact tells us that there are men, of "super-human virtue, a heroic and divine kind of nature." They have immersed themselves in the quest for the divine and for justice on earth. In our time, we may think of Mahatma Gandhi, Nelson Mandela, Mother Teresa, the Dalai Lama, Aung Sun Suu Kyi, or John Paul II. Recognized by many for the eminence of their vision, their goodness, their courage, and their pursuit of justice and truth, they have opened doors to new dimensions in our modern world. They have given history meaning.[3]

To understand Vanier's own thinking about community, the personal good, and the call to be fully human, it is important to recognize the abiding influence of Aristotle on his thought, an indebtedness that goes back to his initial mentoring time with Père Thomas and his brother Marie-Dominique.

But Père Thomas would teach Vanier more than the enlightened rigor of Thomistic and Aristotelian thinking. Distanced from any official position in the order because of persistent suspicions around the orthodoxy of some of his mystical thinking, Père Thomas was exploring new directions of his own through his relationship with the Canadian psychiatrist John Thompson and also with a colleague of Thompson's, Dr. Préaut, whose thinking in the area of mental disabilities was original and attractive. Thompson introduced him to the writings of Carl Gustav Jung and helped shape Père Thomas's thinking around the notion of communion, the primal pact or connection between the mother and the child. Freud's emphasis on sexuality and pathology eclipsed the special beauty of the bond between mother and child. Thanks to Thompson, Père Thomas and Vanier came to attach much significance to this foundational stage of communion. And because of the meeting of minds between Dr. Préaut and Père Thomas, Vanier would come to see the power of grace in an extended communion, a communion that would become the nexus of his life and vocation.

Dr. Préaut, along with M. Prat, the French psychiatrist, established a home and workshop for young men who were mentally disabled in the village of Trosly-Breuil and named it Val Fleuri. Prat was reluctant to place his son who was disabled in a mental institution, so Préaut persuaded him that a home that could accommodate his son and other young men was Val Fleuri, which consisted of an old village château and horse stables but was nicely adjusted to meet the needs of its new and treasured occupants. In addition to recruiting Prat, Préaut also enlisted Père Thomas as the chaplain. The Dominican was willing to do so.

And so with few possessions but with the permission of his superiors, Père Thomas began a journey that would bring him into a world previously unknown to him. Strangely, because of a marked strain of anticlericalism among the other workers at Val Fleuri (many disgruntled ex-seminarians and wannabe candidates that had been turned down) the friar was forced to seek accommodation elsewhere in the village, a situation that he accepted with equanimity. In many ways, his identification with the poor folk of the village helped him in his new ministry. In addition, he would come to see that his work with the mentally challenged young men living in Val Fleuri was the consummate place for him to be following many years of distrust and hardship, a place where those who may be "poor in their head, poor in their person" have an encompassing love for Jesus that couldn't but inspire him.

Père Thomas invited Vanier to visit him in Trosly-Breuil to help him fix the slightly broken-down chapel and to meet his new friends. The priest was his spiritual director and saw something in the ex-navy officer and now freshly minted scholar things that Vanier didn't yet see in himself, including a fresh openness to vulnerability. To encourage him to think along the lines of joining the community of the blessed wounded, Père Thomas welcomed Vanier to a theatrical production put on by the men of Val Fleuri. The experience was as unsettling as it was enlightening. The incipient violence, cacophony, and chaos that accompanied the experience distressed Vanier. He was certainly not persuaded at this point that his future vocation was to be found in Val Fleuri.

Vanier returned to Canada in January of 1964 and accepted a position at the University of St. Michael's College to teach ethics. He quickly discovered two things that marveled him: that the students were far more interested in themes around friendship and sexuality than they were in abstract ethical principles, and that he could teach, teach effectively, and establish very quickly a reputation as a popular instructor.

As rewarding as this position at St. Michael's proved to be, and as enticing as the offer for a permanent appointment was, Vanier felt compelled to return to France and to Père Thomas. In his heart he knew that the both of them were called together by Jesus to do "something," to be present as witnesses to the Gospel in a way that was still unclear but beginning to come into existence.

He came to see that his initial discomfort at Val Fleuri was more his problem than that of the men, that the pain and suffering he saw there were signs of a thirst for love, for friendship, and for communion that he could not ignore.

It was time to reunite with his spiritual master; it was time to return to France.

CHAPTER THREE

L'Arche, the Beginning

Amidst the pain, confusion, panic, and dislocation that Vanier encountered at Val Fleuri. he also discovered God's presence. At the core of the sadness of his new friends, there was a yearning for love, a capacity to give love, and a gift for friendship that needed heeding and cried out for recognition.

Vanier responded to the sacred dream for community for those who were mentally challenged and abandoned by choosing to build a home close to Val Fleuri. With the help of his parents, their mutual friend and social justice activist Tony Walsh (founder of the Benedict Labre House in Montreal), and the Jesuit poet and activist Daniel Berrigan who introduced him to Louis Pretty (an architect and fellow Canadian), Vanier had the materials necessary for the foundation of his new residence: funding, a legal structure, and architectural design.

On August 4, 1964, "L'Arche," the Ark, was born, sans electricity (although Vanier would later discover the electric meter), sans plumbing, but *with* a special beauty and simplicity.

The first inhabitants, besides Vanier, would include three men—Raphaël, Philippe, and Dany—all previous residents of St. Jean les Deux Jumeaux, an asylum for those who were intellectually disabled. Vanier's housemates, but more importantly his brothers, constituted a unique kind of community. The first night in their residence went well for three of them, but Dany found the unfamiliar surroundings deeply distressing. His inability to communicate was exacerbated by the foreign environment, emotional turmoil, and hallucinations that imperiled his welfare and the future of the project.

He needed to be returned to St. Jean. This loss, their first community pain, was a stark reminder to Vanier that the romanticism of poverty, struggle, and desperate suffering was merely a sheen, a gloss, easily scoured by a raw encounter with human weakness and fear. Community could not be established by fiat; it is built on blood, tears, resolve, and unremitting love. Sturdy stuff and not the fluff of heroic dreaming.

Biographer Spink puts it well when she notes of these early days of L'Arche:

> Despite the barrier of pre-conceived ideas and psychological defense mechanisms that he was obliged to recognize existed even within himself, Vanier began to realize that he had everything to discover about people with disabilities. . . . During those first months he learned a great deal, not least that Raphaël and Philippe did not want to live with a retired naval officer who ordered them about and thought himself superior. Nor did they want to live with an ex-professor of philosophy who thought he knew all the right theories. He had left the naval world where weakness was something to be shunned at all costs and joined a different world at Eau Vive, the world of thought where once again weakness, ignorance and incompetence were things to be shunned. Life with Raphaël and Philippe moved him into a world of poverty, weakness and fragility

in a way which supplemented his ideas and theories about human beings with the discovery of what is meant to be really human.[1]

It wasn't going to be an easy trip, this journey into the deeper meaning of life, and it wasn't going to be without its obstacles, frustrations, moments of stunned incomprehension, and days of dark disappointment. But it would be a journey into the light for all that, a journey into greater humanization, a journey defined by periodic agapaic epiphanies.

From the outset Vanier was determined to tell the story of L'Arche to solicit funds and support from like-minded people, to heighten awareness of the life of people who were disabled, to bring into conversation and commitment those on the periphery, and to deepen the understanding of those at the core. One practical way he did this was the circular letter. The first appeared on August 22, eighteen days after the opening of the home in Trosly-Breuil, and succinctly articulates the philosophy of L'Arche:

> L'Arche is convinced that if the handicapped are unable to find their stability in modern society, which is becoming more and more complicated with its bureaucracy and techniques, they can find true human and spiritual growth in a family-like environment. L'Arche wants to create homes where life is focused on service to those who are the poorest of the poor in this twentieth century. L'Arche does not want to be a center where those who have been rejected are simply kept or cared for; it wants to be a place where they can truly grow and develop according to their specific qualities and capacities.
>
> L'Arche is a Catholic home. It believes that if those who are handicapped cannot be educated or work in the same way as others do, they are nevertheless open to spiritual

values. Their very poverty is a pre-disposition to receive the graces of love that Jesus has promised them. L'Arche homes are open to all those who suffer, without any distinction of class, culture or religion; religious practice is entirely optional.[2]

The ecumenical and interfaith foundation of L'Arche is significant on several fronts: The Second Vatican Council—an ecumenical council—was in the penultimate year of its convocation with much still to happen. An openness to other doctrinal and spiritual traditions was a supreme rarity in the Catholic world. The bold declaration of welcome to all willing to share in the foundation's vision irrespective of canonical status, gender, religious outlook and formation was a harbinger of subsequent developments that would flourish in the post-conciliar period.

At the core of the L'Arche vision is the personal, the relational, and the biographical. For all of his training in the science of philosophy, Vanier never loses the prime importance of the individual response, the emotional interaction, and the power of the heart. Certainly his service to Philippe and to Raphaël—and to the countless others who would come to be associated with the L'Arche family—was shaped by a Christian humanism, a gospel-centeredness, that spoke to the universal in all of us. But it started with the personal, and that remains the foundation. What Vanier learned in his early days with Philippe and Raphaël would be the flesh to his theory:

> As I began to live with Philippe and Raphaël, the first thing I discovered was the depth of their pain, the pain of having been a disappointment for their parents and others. One can understand their parents' reaction to them. What parents would not be distressed, grief filled or even angry to

discover that their child would never be able to talk, walk or live like others? Parents whose children have disabilities suffer deeply, but their children who have the disabilities suffer deeply, too. Raphaël and Philippe had incredibly sensitive hearts. They had been deeply wounded and humiliated by rejection, and by the lack of consideration shown them by those around them. Because of this, they sometimes became very angry, or escaped into a world of dreams. It was quite clear that they had a great need for friendship and trust, and to be able to express their needs to somebody who would really listen. For far too long, nobody had been interested in listening to them or in helping them make choices and become more responsible for their lives. In fact, their needs were exactly the same as mine: *to be loved and to love, to make choices and to develop their abilities* [my italics].[3]

It was not that the first two companions were a test case, an easy template for the future, specimens for an argument. Rather, the personal encounter, the personal observations, and the personal insights garnered from this unlikely trinity became the primal truth validating the charism, lifting above sociological data, psychological analysis, and theological imperatives the human need for solidarity and community:

Making friends with Raphaël and Philippe and living a covenant, a sacred bond, with them implied an enormous change in the way I approached life. My education had taught me to be quick and efficient, and to make my own decisions. I was, first and foremost, a man of action rather than a man who listened. In the navy, I had colleagues, but no real friends. Opening ourselves to friendship means becoming vulnerable, taking off our masks and letting down our barriers so that we can accept people just as they are, with all their beauty and gifts as well as their weaknesses and inner wounds. It means weeping with them when they weep and laughing when they laugh. I had created barriers around my heart to protect it from pain. In L'Arche, I was no longer climbing the ladder of human promotion and becoming more and more efficient and important. Instead I was "descending," "wasting time" with people with intellectual disabilities, so that together we could create communities, places of covenant and communion.[4]

What Philippe and Raphaël did for Vanier was to awaken the "qualities of the heart, the child within," and in doing so empowered the philosopher and naval officer, the thinker and the doer, to negotiate a new way of being present, of being in the world—a way of listening and attending with intentional vulnerability. Reciprocity, mutuality, and interdependency would now become key features of Vanier's vocation as a Christian: not only to identify with the poor and broken as objects of sympathy and good works but far more radically to enter their world through shared life, eliminating hierarchy and status, and touched by the grace and goodness of their lives as felt and experienced in community.

Very quickly—within a year of the founding of L'Arche—new challenges to leadership would emerge as Val Fleuri required Vanier to become its new director following a crisis of direction and personnel. The numbers increased, the pressures of budget planning mounted, and the politics of sustaining an expanding community with limited economic possibilities necessitated working closely with all kinds of medical professionals, social workers, and government bureaucrats. They accepted a number of young disabled boys, especially those with no parents or with guardians to see to their care.

Vanier wrote in a circular letter of November 5, 1965, that they needed to "create a centre where our boys can grow and develop according to their human and spiritual capacities, where they can be happy, work and receive the education that corresponds to their needs, where they can be encouraged to use their leisure hours in a beneficial way and be helped medically and psychologically. Finally, they need to feel that they are at home, 'en famille,' in the security that flows from love."[5]

Embarked then on an undertaking that would change his life and the life of the others close to him, on a pastoral experiment, a gospel-inspired project of undifferentiating love and compassion, Vanier and L'Arche were unfolding with confidence and vision.

But as important as the particulars around this development, the very conception of L'Arche as a response to God's call, and the key personalities involved in facilitating it being established are, there is an intellectual and spiritual background to L'Arche that is neatly outlined by biographer Spink:

Not only was there the influence of Catherine Doherty's Friendship House and Tony Walsh's Benedict Labre House as communities based very much on pain, mercy and welcome, in which lay people lived a life of simplicity and poverty with the very poor, but in 1954, in Montreal, Jean Vanier had come to know the Little Sisters of Jesus and their fraternity based on the spirituality of Charles de Foucauld. L'Arche would come to feel very close to the Little Sisters and Brothers over the years, discovering a common basis in the Spirituality of Nazareth, the recognition of Jesus present in the poor, the simplicity of their daily life and the quest for unity. Eau Vive had undoubtedly also left its mark, although there for Jean Vanier it had been more a question of discovering the ways of the Spirit in the sense of trying to be faithful to what Jesus wanted. Dorothy Day's paper, the *Catholic Worker,* had made a profound impression on him. He had also visited the Foyer de Charité begun by Cardinal Leger in Montreal. There people with physical and mental disabilities were welcomed in a spirit of prayer. Elements of all these would find their way into L'Arche.[6]

A desert spirituality, a radical commitment to the poor, a high premium placed on the charisms of hospitality and humility, and a communal incarnation of the gift of simplicity—all these are the ingredients that compose the core L'Arche vision and represent the broad infusion of ideas, the open reciprocity of gift, and the generous interchange of support and solidarity that define the Catholic sensibility at its best.

Very quickly the L'Arche movement expanded, new houses opened, the international dimension underscored, and the philosophy and ethos skillfully refined.

Vanier saw the L'Arche community having two distinctive objectives. First, homes had to be created for the psychologically and physically wounded allowing for a "new autonomy." Vanier insisted we must all remember that in addition to the "primary wound," there are the other and often far graver wounds of marginalization, indifference, and condescension. People who are disabled or challenged are often made to feel unwanted, inferior, or a nuisance rather than a joy. The best way of doing that, reasoned Vanier, is by encouragement, building confidence in the face of rejection, and recognizing the value of the weak in a world that only worships the "strong," however that is defined.

The second distinctive objective is the community-building thrust of L'Arche homes. Such a community does not stand in judgment of others or allocate value on the basis of utility, but attaches primacy to love and not personal pleasure or self-aggrandizement.

Vanier notes "the pedagogy of the heart must go beyond our personal egoism and open us up more to the sufferings of others." An experience with L'Arche is an experience in self-emptying, selfless service, and genuine community. Such high rhetoric could be seen as pious exhortation, a summons to the ideal life encased in a noble sheen but out of touch with the real world, but it is that real world that interests Vanier—the real world of muck, mire, blood, despair, and struggle; the real world in which people are discarded because they are not productive; the real world that has little patience for the broken; the real world that crucified divinity and aches for redemption.

CHAPTER FOUR

A Death and an Inspiration

L'Arche is a real world *living* in a real world; it is no place for heroic fantasies, ephemeral romance, or provisional commitment.

There was nothing provisional about Vanier's personal commitment. He was, and remains, in for the long haul. But at the same time as he was fully engaged in securing a sound footing for L'Arche, navigating the rip tides of a radical venture, and working out the minutiae of financial autonomy, Vanier found himself witness to his father's dying—both a profound grace and a deep pain.

Writer and biographer Mary Frances Coady describes the scene of the governor general's passing with its attendant players, quiet dignity, and solemn protocol:

> The chaplain, Father Hermas Guindon, arrived at ten-thirty for morning Mass. Pauline was already in the bedroom with her husband, as were their sons Jean, who had come to Canada on a lecture tour, and Michel. Dr. Burton [Georges's doctor] had also arrived. Father Guindon brought communion, and then Pauline and her sons went into the chapel for Mass. When the patient indicated that

his oxygen mask was irritating and tried to remove it, Sergeant Chevrier [Georges's valet] wiped it out and then gently replaced it and gave him a sip of water. Georges said a faint "Merci." By the time the family returned to his bedside, he was already dying. Dr. Burton felt his pulse becoming increasingly weaker, and quietly announced at eleven twenty-two that he was dead.[1]

It was March 3, 1967, Canada's centennial year, and its governor general would not survive it. But what did survive is Georges's profound and sustained influence on his son. Jean recognized in his father a singular humility, especially in light of his vice-regal position and with his distinguished record of diplomatic and military service: "In no way did he let the honours which people piled upon him go to his head. It was accurately said of him that he accepted them in spite of himself; certainly they left him not a whit less sensitive to the needs and sufferings of others. In his heart of hearts he considered himself no more than a lowly servant of God, as the signature of one of his letters bears witness."[2]

Jean valued his father's simplicity of faith unencumbered by frivolous ratiocination, ecclesiastical battles, or by squabbles among systematic theologians:

Without faith nothing made sense to my father. It was as simple as that. It was hardly surprising that he felt no need for theological propositions. With youthful pretensions, I would sometimes put to him some new theological thoughts. "That must be very interesting," he would say and add with a mischievous twinkle, "perhaps you should tell it to your mother." So direct was his own faith— diamond-like said Cardinal Leger—that he felt no need to be clouded with unspiritual considerations or fine points of doctrine or dogma. So complete was it that no contentious evidence or sad calamities could shake it. "We cannot know the meaning of innocent suffering or calamity," he would say, "but we know that God is love and therefore all these things which happen must happen for some purpose and in the end all work out for the best."[3]

And Jean was inspired by his father's deep sense of love for others and the concomitant sense of service that such love generates:

In his relations with others my father seems to have found towards the end of his life a remarkable balance between his spiritual life, his simple but radiant capacity to give of himself, and his undoubted sense of duty. As a young man he had shown himself to be a person of virtue and courage, with a clear sense of justice; later in life, his interior and spiritual life developed, and he became a man of prayer. Finally at Rideau Hall [official residence of the governor-general of Canada] this interior life, rooted in his sense of justice, expanded into a simple and sensitive love for all. He underlined in the writings of Charles de Foucauld the passages where the author tells of his desire to be a "universal brother." At the end of his life, I think my father aspired to just this.[4]

Humility, faith, and love were the ingredients of his father's faith and the seeds of Jean's own. The year 1967 was one for grieving but also one of expanding horizons. The work and vision of L'Arche would bring Vanier, core members, and assistants on a pilgrimage to many of the Marian shrines of France, Spain, and Portugal: La Salette, Lourdes, Montserrat, and Fatima. This journey to the sites of Marian apparitions was not simply an exercise in popular piety, because Vanier does not despise the robust and often visceral devotionalism associated with the cult of Mary, but rather they were journeys that sought to better understand and channel the special relationship Christians have with Mary.

The witness of Mary, her brave fiat, the heroic subversiveness of the *Magnificat*, her centrality in salvation history, and her modeling of the virtues of true discipleship have found expression in Vanier's many writings over the years, maturing and deepening as a consequence of his evolving ecumenical and interreligious interests.

Mary was there at the beginning; she is the heart of the L'Arche prayer:

> O Mary,
> we ask you to bless our house,
> keep it in your immaculate heart,
> make L'Arche a true home,
> a refuge for the poor, the little ones,
> so that here they may find the source of all life,
> a refuge for those who are deeply tried,
> so that they may find your infinite consolation.
> O Mary,
> give us hearts that are attentive,
> humble and gentle,
> so that we may welcome with tenderness and compassion
> all the poor you send us.
> Give us hearts full of compassion
> so that we can love, serve,
> dissolve all discord,
> and see in our suffering and broken brothers the humble presence
> of Jesus.[5]

Of special importance over the years is the shrine at Lourdes, a sacred place where the maimed, the broken, the ill, and the dying come for consolation, for mercy, for hope. It was here where Vanier and a French woman, Marie-Hélène Matthieu, resolved to hold international pilgrimages for people with disabilities, along with their family and friends; it would be a pilgrimage of inclusion, solidarity, and rejoicing. Vanier argued that the very idea of pilgrimage, *peregrinatio* (or going forth into strange lands), was key to understanding religious yearning—Jewish, Muslim, Hindu, and Christian—and that it should be a time of inclusion.

The groups that organized these Lourdes pilgrimages came to the conclusion that the times they had together—the socializing, the bonding, the praying—should not die when the pilgrimage ended but in some way continue. That "way" became known as the Faith and Light communities, and they are now scattered in the hundreds throughout the world.

As the momentum for the establishment of L'Arche foyers and Faith and Light communities gathered steam, the demands on Vanier's time for speaking, advocating, and fundraising increased proportionately. He began to see his personal limitations against a backdrop of severe poverty, monumental struggle, and human incapacity—and nowhere was that more in evidence than in India. In a letter written to friends from Calcutta (now Kolkata) on November 25, 1972, Vanier poignantly notes:

> I was shaken by the poverty I saw. It is so easy to reject the poor. So many times I have done it simply because I did not quite know what to do. It is easy to reject someone begging for money to buy a coffee and yet we easily stop and have a coffee ourselves when we really do not need it; our stomachs are full and our pockets too! We always want to be "reasonable" and refuse any extreme situations or gestures; yet if we want to follow Jesus, we have to follow exactly what he says! I spoke to Mother Teresa's novices and sisters, about three hundred of them in all. It is easy to speak about Jesus, Jesus in the poor; but to go out into the streets and come face to face with people in rags, people with empty stomachs, is another matter. Pray that I may

learn how to live with the poor and never let my heart be closed up in my own comfort, well-being or flattery. Pray that Jesus may keep me continually in anguish in front of the poor.[6]

This radical and Franciscan identification with the poor—laced with Kierkegaardian earnestness—will become the dominant and defining motif of Vanier's thinking. A major influence in shaping this identification is Blessed Mother Teresa. They first met in the United States when they were both receiving the Joseph Kennedy Foundation Award, and it was clear at the outset that there was much that they shared in common.

Mother Teresa, founder of the Missionaries of Charity, "God's pencil" as she called herself, servant of the poorest of the poor and consoler of the dying, was during her lifetime a model of holiness that admitted to no redeeming vices. She was fiercely obedient and fiercely demanding in obedience, driven, disinclined to nuance and compromise, contemptuous of political propriety, and prepared to fix her sail to whatever ship of disrepute floated by as long as God's forsaken were touched by love in the end. Mother Teresa was not that much different from other headstrong saints of the past, except whereas many of the confessors, martyrs, and virtuous women of history had their struggles with church officialdom, labored under the shadow of disapproval, and knew the bitter taste of failure and obscurity, Mother Teresa seemed to have the papal Good Housekeeping™ seal of approval from the outset and basked in the rays of global affirmation. She was a star in her own time.

But she could be a prick to an uneasy conscience. While many individuals, agencies, and governments lacked either the determination or the resources to redress the egregious wrongs of society or felt immobilized by the sheer magnitude of the task, Mother Teresa had no problems galloping in where a legion of angels dared not tread. She cajoled government officials, badgered diffident if not exhausted relief workers, prodded religious women and men to make greater sacrifices, connived with business and political leaders to get things done even as they sought to use her for some specious legitimacy, and insisted on controlling her media image. She had little time for theological and philosophical dissent, neither grasped nor indicated any desire to understand current issues like feminism, subscribed unconditionally to a traditionalist reading of the natural law theory, disregarded the determinative role of political ideologies in the shaping of systems and nations, and was passionate about only one "industry"—love of the poorest of the poor.

In a time when many are skittish about claiming God's alliance with human projects; when the ominous theocratization of secular politics in both democratic and nondemocratic regimes has many frightened; when the invocation of God's blessings on crusades and jihads against causes, governments, and people judged as infidels or apostates continues unabated; and when the proliferation of ultraconservative spokespersons in the media and through well-funded lobbying forces seems beyond termination, Mother Teresa can look suspect. Was she one of "them"?

In the eyes of some, Mother Teresa's certainty damns her. In the eyes of others, she represents, either willingly or unintentionally, a type of woman that is premodern. For her admirers, and their number is legion, and for her apologists, and their number is markedly less, Mother Teresa is simply Mother, endlessly giving, radically committed to Jesus, one signed with love.

This is the Teresa that interested and inspired Vanier—the one signed with love. A sophisticated thinker, well trained in the nuances and subtleties of interpretation, fearful of any iteration of dogmatic or moral absolutism, and distrustful of both the unchecked fervor of zealots and the easy deference of the devout to institutional totalism, Vanier's intellectual formation, privileged upbringing, and undemonstrative and quiet leadership stand in sharp contrast to the Macedonian *beata*.

But he shared with her a magnanimity of spirit, a fearless advocacy for the marginalized, and an inexhaustible energy for God's work. They may well have thought differently, but their affections were aligned, their teleological intentions convergent, and their capacity for service in love illimitable.

CHAPTER FIVE

Growing Internationalism

Throughout the 1970s, international interest in both L'Arche and the Faith and Light communities grew enormously. It was a welcome contagion of love and vision, and Vanier traveled extensively to meet, consult, organize, and inspire the many new beginnings that were unfolding at breakneck speed. In addition to new places in both Canada and the United States, Vanier clocked up the miles visiting India, Haiti, Italy, Australia, New Zealand, the Republic of Ireland, Northern Ireland, Honduras, Brazil, Ivory Coast, Israel, Lebanon, Poland, Papua New Guinea, Guatemala, Belgium, France, the United Kingdom, and Scandinavia.

This explosive growth required vigilance, planning, and spiritual sustenance. It also required a superhuman energy that could spend itself in exhaustion and leave Vanier exposed to a weakened system and infection. In 1976 it happened. He was admitted to Cochin Hospital in Paris following his return from a visit to India with a rising fever, recurring diarrhea, and significant depletion of energy. The hospital physicians concluded that he had amoebic hepatitis, and he began an antibiotic regimen designed to fight the

disease. A long period of hospital and post-hospital conva-
lescence began. As usual, Vanier drew the right lessons:

> I am writing once again from the hospital. Alleluia! Since
> my last letter many beautiful things have happened. . . .
> Through all this Jesus is teaching me patience. The doctors
> have no idea when all this will be finished nor when I can
> leave the hospital nor whether I will need a long period of
> convalescence. Jesus is teaching me just to live day by day,
> happy to be where I am for the moment, happy to fulfill
> the vocation of today. There are, of course, moments of
> anguish, but I quickly ask Jesus to chase them away and
> to fill my heart with thanksgiving and trust. Is it not St.
> Paul in his letter to the Philippians who says: "Rejoice in
> the Lord always, again I say to you Rejoice." I have much
> to rejoice about, in particular the love of my brothers and
> sisters all over the world. There are so many who are sup-
> porting me in this new vocation which will last. Père
> Thomas has been particularly good; his quiet, prayerful
> presence helps me to be abandoned, quiet and silent inte-
> riorly (from circular letter dated April 27, 1976).[1]

Following his period of rest and recovery, Vanier resumed
his earlier responsibilities as director of L'Arche in Trosly-
Breuil as well as his traveling. While in Tegucigalpa, the
capital of Honduras, he wrote a letter for the worldwide
community that underlined his love for the poor—a growing preoccupation that does not diminish in time—and be-
trays his anxieties around the functions of the assistants as
opposed to the core or permanent members of the L'Arche
houses:

> I personally feel I have a lot to learn from Latin America.
> Nowhere else in the world have I felt with such force the
> gap that exists between the rich, those who possess, and

the poor, who live in total insecurity. . . . Is it possible to create in Latin America small Christian communities which could be like yeast in the dough and at the heart of which would be the poorest and the most rejected?

Everything I see here makes me really question our L'Arche communities and the double culture of the "assistants" and the "assisted" that can exist, the danger that can arise when the "assistants" possess power and security, and benefit from the "assisted" in order to gain a certain prestige. The more I advance in age, the more I discover how much I must grow more deeply in humility, which Jesus alone can give me. In order to do that, I need a truly loving and demanding community. I also need to live with and listen to the poorest and weakest ones. How easily we can fall into hypocrisy and verbalism. L'Arche can only exist if the "assistants" die to the culture of our times so that others can leave their culture of sadness and despair and be reborn; together we can create a new culture, which is also the oldest culture, founded on love and a faithful commitment to one another, a love that is ever new and renewed in and through Jesus.[2]

Again and again throughout his life and ministry, Vanier has subjected to scrutiny his motives, his failures, and his dependency on the love and grace of others. It is not enough to establish a structure and then leave it to function without the rigorous honesty and transparency of an institutional *particular examen*. It is not enough to remain safely distant from the dynamic of learning that shapes, unnerves, and challenges us on a daily basis. It is not enough to have an attitude and a work strategy that prioritizes the poor because to be truly servants of the poor we must have our hearts broken by them. It is not enough to aspire to humility as it must enter into our very blood and sinew, our very being, not a spiritual affectation or pose we assume, but a disposition of heart that defines us.

Touched by the desperation of Latin America as well as by its enormous spiritual potential, Vanier would find himself, like many others in the world, stunned by the professional assassination of the archbishop of San Salvador, Honduras's bloodied neighbor, one Oscar Arnulfo Romero.

The world was upended when Romero was gunned down while saying Mass on March 24, 1980. It was barely a day after Romero had been identified as an enemy of the state by the powerful politician Major Roberto D'Aubuisson, founder of the Nationalist Republican Alliance Party or ARENA. Romero had provoked D'Aubuisson and his ilk after giving a stirring sermon calling on soldiers, as Christians, to choose God's imperative not to kill over the government's repeated and increasingly aggressive violations of human rights.

By training and temperament a conservative churchman, Romero had been hesitant to denounce the government on human rights infractions because of his fear of unlawful insurgency. He was inclined, as is the case with the majority of Roman prelates, to view the spirit of revolution with fear if not detestation. The overthrow of legitimate authority, irrespective of the genuine abuses of that authority by those exercising power, is the court of last resort. Rome abominates the usurpation of established authority, most especially since 1848, the "year of revolutions," with the subsequent self-incarceration of Pope Pius IX in 1870 following the final annexation of the Papal City States by the Italian Nationalists. Still, the Roman Catholic tradition does allow for a revolutionary uprising should all the conditions apply: "a manifest, and long-standing tyranny which would do great damage to fundamental personal rights and dangerous harm to the common good of the country" as written in *Populo-rum Progressio* by Pope Paul VI (March 26, 1967).

Arguably, such a state of affairs existed in El Salvador during the leadership of Romero, but the archbishop would never have adopted a policy in favor of violent insurrection. His preferred path was that of Christian nonviolence, and he came to this choice—of nonviolent opposition to governing powers and their allies—after the death of his adviser Rutilio Grande, a Jesuit. Grande's death sealed in blood Romero's resolve to actively and explicitly oppose government malfeasance.

Vanier was a keen and sympathetic admirer of Romero, having been several times to Latin America, including El Salvador, and tasting firsthand the bloody persecutions and systematic violence in the Catholic Americas. Vanier was in Choluteca, Honduras, when Romero was killed, and he was asked to preach the homily in the city's cathedral at the official Mass to be offered for the slain shepherd. He observed later in a letter that "It was a grace for me to speak of Romero who, like Jesus, was not afraid to speak the truth, again and again. I am full of admiration for the church of Latin America, which is beginning to flourish in its commitment to the poor and where there are so many men and women full of courage and truth, prepared to risk their lives. The documents of Medellín and Puebla, which reflect the thoughts of the Latin American church, are important for us and for the entire Church."[3]

Vanier's familiarity with the key CELAM conferences (the council of bishops throughout Latin America) and with their innovative and yet radical documents that became foundation stones for the church's wider conscientization around issues of poverty, marginality, Christian witness, martyrdom, and the building of the reign of God, reminds us that though he was a tireless activist, Vanier was richly nourished by the thinking of the church, au courant with the controversies and policies swirling around him and a discerning reader of the "signs of the times."

The year 1980 was a watershed one in other respects as well. Since the founding of L'Arche in 1964, the journey was no simple trajectory. There were many curves, detours, a few roundabouts, and occasionally a straight boulevard. It was a journey into the unknown, a journey that would see Vanier's own involvement change with shifting priorities. He recounts in *An Ark for the Poor: The Story of L'Arche*:

> In 1978 we opened a new house in Trosly, la Forestière, where we welcomed Eric, Yvan, Edith, Marie-Jo, and six others. Each one had severe intellectual disabilities; none of them could talk, and their independence was very limited. I had started L'Arche with people who had a certain independence: they could work in the workshops. A few even left to live independently in their own apartments in Compiègne. As group homes and workshops organized by various parents' associations started to develop in France, we began to realize the pain and rejection of those who were more severely disabled. They were too limited to fit into a workshop program or be welcomed into group homes.
>
> La Forestière brought a whole new dimension to L'Arche: the discovery of the presence of God hidden in the hearts of those who are *extremely* [my italics] poor and weak. . . . In 1980, when I left the responsibility as leader of the Trosly community, I asked Odile, who replaced me as Director, and the community council, if I could live and work for a year at la Forestière. That year with Eric, Lucien, and the others was important for me. I discovered the great capacity for relationship of these men and women who were very limited on the rational and verbal level. They

were extremely poor intellectually, but tremendously rich in qualities of the heart. For us to perceive all the treasure of their hearts, we ourselves must become poor; we have to move into a slower pace of life, be more attentive, more centered and more contemplative. They invite us to an interior silence in order to welcome them within their silence.

After sixteen years of responsibility in the community and on the international level, I had to let go of my desires for efficiency and learn how to "waste time" in simple, loving relationships. I learned a great deal during that year, and my heart was transformed. I rediscovered the deep meaning of L'Arche. I also touched the powers of darkness hidden within my heart and experienced more deeply my own poverty. When we live day after day with people who are severely disabled, our own limits and darkness are revealed. This experience helped me understand that we cannot grow in love and compassion unless, in all truth, we recognize who we are and accept our own radical poverty. The poor person is not just in others, but also within us. That truth is the basis of all human and spiritual growth and the foundation of our Christian life. "Blessed are the poor in spirit, for theirs is the kingdom of heaven" (Matthew 5:3). The poor, who reveal our poverty to us, thus become a sacrament.[4]

For Vanier, 1980 brought him closer to the agony of Latin America, the agony of his own spiritual inadequacy, and the redeeming agony of the profoundly challenged.

A philosopher by training and nature, and a well-read spiritual theologian by election, Vanier always looks for the right synthesis, the coming together of theory and praxis, the commingling of faith and reason.

The injustices rampant in Latin America, the heroicity of virtue, as the Roman canonists would phrase it, of those women and men prepared to lay down their lives in service of the Way, the Truth, and the Life, spoke directly to the mission of L'Arche itself.

But that mission could be seen with some anxiety, misconstrued and sidelined by church authorities fearful of the blurring of denominational lines.

CHAPTER SIX

Vanier and Wojtyla

Although L'Arche began life with a distinctly Catholic flavor, a Eucharistic tonality, a gospel-mandated urgency, and founded by Catholics—a Dominican theologian and a lay philosopher—from the outset it was ecumenical in its reach. In time, it would be interfaith, fully *catholic*, inclusive, and open, but never at the cost of its authentic origins and abiding vision.

Some in Rome, particularly in the Pontifical Council for the Laity, had difficulties with Vanier's perceived fudging on the issue of definition. He was encouraged to declare decisively whether L'Arche was or was not a Roman Catholic community. Vanier was pleased with and supportive of the direction L'Arche had been taking for some time, which was to be genuinely ecumenical and interfaith, and was distressed by the insistence of some Roman functionaries to define L'Arche in more exclusively Catholic and canonical terms.

However, when the Argentine cardinal Eduardo Pironio (one time *papabile* and now a Servant of God, the first stage in the process of sainting) was appointed President of the Pontifical Council, relations with the Vatican improved considerably. Friendship and trust rather than caution and suspicion were now the order of the day.

The professional and fraternal relationship Vanier had with Pironio would soon blossom to include Pironio's boss: Pope St. John Paul II.

Invited to participate as a lay delegate at the 1987 episcopal synod on the "Vocation and Mission of the Lay Faithful in the Church and in the World Twenty Years after the Second Vatican Council," which would not have been issued without the express validation of the pontiff, Vanier found himself at the heart of the Roman machinery of government—Curia and synod assembly, all with pronounced papal oversight.

He notes in a letter the month before the Roman Synod—September 29, 1987:

> While in Chicago, I received a telephone call from the Apostolic Nuncio in Ottawa telling me I had been invited by John Paul II to the Synod on the Laity. I believe it was the Canadian bishops who submitted my name. I will be in Rome for the whole month of October. I had to cancel retreats I was supposed to give in Poland and in Winnipeg. I am sorry about these changes, but I am happy to be going to the Synod in the name of L'Arche and of Faith and Light. I feel I am going there to represent those who have no voice, those who could never assume a role on the level of the universal church and yet are at the heart of that church for they are hidden in the heart of God. I want to go to the Synod as a child, to receive all that Jesus wants to give me and also to give what Jesus wants me to give. Pray for me and for the Synod.[1]

There is, perhaps, a certain naïve dimension to Vanier's almost sheep-like innocence regarding the synod, its process, its politics, and its effectiveness for the church universal. As is characteristic of his approach to church leaders, to those in authority, and to those who exercise specific ministries, he attributes the very best to their motives, does not second-guess their intentions, and recognizes the problems that do surface are as a result of human structures and patterns of behavior that run counter to the operations of grace. He writes in a letter that follows the first week of the synod that "there is a real consensus of faith, but often in practice there are blockages that come from different attitudes or from fear of relationship and cooperation which prevent this participation.

The most important blockage in his view is the myopic attitude of many of the synod Fathers who, although freely and generously

> talking about the participation of lay people in the decision-making and mission of the Church, few talk about the important place of the poor. The Latin American bishops are the most outspoken with regard to the preferential option for the poor and basic Christian communities with the poor. It is true that the participation of lay people in the responsibility of the Church is a real source of wealth for the Church, but there is the other aspect of going down the ladder in order to live and share one's life with the poor. I sense that that is the call of L'Arche: *to live and share with people who have limited capacities and who will never be able to take on responsibility* [italics added].

> John Paul II is at every session. I spend much of my time watching him, especially the way he listens to each speaker. He listens very intensely; he does not say a word. He is truly a model for us.[2]

At the heart of the synod's proceedings was a lengthy but hardly contested discussion of the ecclesiological notion of *communio*. Although debates around the meaning of the word, its nuances and implications, seemed largely confined to corridor discussion among the episcopal delegates, the unanimity exhibited in the synod hall was illustrative of the tight control over discussion and debates exercised by the very pontiff Vanier saw as a model of attention and openness. It was very clear, if not from the outset certainly at the conclusion of the synod, that the role and charism of the laity are not to be found encroaching ministerial territory, and that the ontological difference between the lay as opposed to the clerical vocation must be clear and emphatically underscored.

In fact, the pope's final homily to the synod delegates makes specific reference to the priestly, kingly, and prophetic dignity that derives from Christ, but those characteristics, Douglas R. Letson (a Canadian journalist and academic credentialed by the press office of the Holy See as a bona fide commentator) rightly observes:

> are related to the Church, not to the laity; moreover the Pope mentions the special covenant that unites the "church-communion," a communion exercised with all the baptized, but nowhere in the midst of these hints to the Book of Exodus or the First Letter of Peter is there any indication that the laity enjoy a type of priesthood. As for the mission of the laity, it resides in the "secular dimension," which is common to all the baptized. How different are the implications from the *intervention* (prepared speech by bishop-delegates) by Donat Chiasson of Moncton, New Brunswick, who became the *enfant terrible* (and the darling of the press) by insisting that the Synod had been hijacked by the hierarchy. Articulating the position of the Canadian delegation, Chiasson, like John Paul II, also talked about the *communio* that derives from one's baptism; but, unlike John Paul II, Chiasson hastened to add that the differing

types of service "do not set up higher or lower classes among the People of God."[3]

Letson's critique of the synod's resistance to genuine consultation was especially charged by the assembly's reluctance to deal directly with the challenges posed by women in ministry. The Canadian bishops were persistent—their critics would argue truculent and disrespectful, or at best impolitic—in raising the vexatious issue of women in the church, their empowerment, their evolving roles, and their cries for full recognition.

Jean-Guy Hamelin, acting in his capacity as President of the Canadian Conference of Catholic Bishops, spoke both forcefully and eloquently in an October 9 intervention. In his address, entitled "God's Humanity: Male and Female," Hamelin made it clear that the participation of women in the life of the church had been strongly addressed during his delegation's preparatory consultations. Hamelin challenged the synod to be more open to expanding women's horizons in the church, pointing out that there is an apparent discrepancy between the roles that women play in society and in the church, and that the discrepancy is particularly difficult to explain to young people. The women's movement in Canada, Hamelin insists, appears to be an evolution toward "justice, dignity, and partnership." But, because women are excluded from the decision-making life of the church, the church, therefore, needs to remove whatever obstacles it can to open positions of responsibility to the laity, to men and women. And as for the question of women's ordination, Hamelin adds, "we cannot avoid underlining in this assembly that the reasoning used so far to explain the reservation of sacred orders to men has not seemed convincing, especially not to young people."[4]

While theologians and reporters, bishops and *periti*, wrestled with the implications of various reports that were not given the airing they merited, while Vatican officials attempted to keep the lid on topics they deemed incendiary, and while the pope attended nearly all sessions and observed what constituted a series of monologues, Vanier remained above the fray. Uninterested in ecclesiastical power plays, his focus remained on the core theological insight of the synod—*communio:*

> Through the different reports, I sense a desire for the Church to become more and more the people of God, the mystical body, where all the followers of Jesus, lay people and priests, work together for the Kingdom. The Church is communion and this is lived out in family, in community and in the parish—which is the community of communities. . . . The Synod confirmed me in the vision of L'Arche as a sign of the Kingdom. But isn't this also a challenge for each one of our communities? It means learning to accept others in their differences and also accepting that our communities can become communities only when people are allowed to exercise their various gifts. However, it is not always easy to welcome differences. So often difference is seen more as a threat than a treasure. Yes, I sense that L'Arche is one of these new communities that the Holy Spirit is calling forth in the Church today.[5]

While the controversies, muzzlings, pent-up frustration, and aura of intrigue are swirling about the synod and its month-long proceedings, Vanier focuses on the centrality of ideas, the global networking, and the gradual process of conscientization. It is not that he is indifferent to the politics or even unaware; it is rather that he refuses to be distracted from the graced moments, the pastoral opportunities, and the deeper prioritizing.

It is in his relationship with John Paul II that one can see *how* Vanier sees a way to underscore the mission of L'Arche. And that relationship will undergo many permutations, refinements, and deepening(s) in the years to come.

Almost a decade after Vanier's time at the Synod of the Laity he received an invitation to speak at a celebration of the new ecclesial movements that proliferated under the Karol Wojtyla papacy.

Although some of these ecclesial movements, many of which have the juridical status of secular institutes, predate the Second Vatican Council (1962–65), all of them greatly prospered in numbers, influence, and power during the reign of John Paul II. These movements—although largely lay in composition, many have clerics specifically ordained to serve their membership—include the highly influential Opus Dei, Communion and Liberation, the Neo-Catechumenate, Focolare, Faith, Miles Jesu, Community of the Beatitudes, and many others. Most of them are conservative, pietistic, scrupulously loyal to the pope, well versed in the laws and traditions of the church, intelligent, sincere, and tireless in expending their energies in the interests of institutional Catholicism. Some are more prophetic in their origins and thrust, like the San Egidio Community:

> San Egidio is a lay community which began in 1968 when ten high school students, most of them baptized but non-practising Roman Catholics, started to read scripture together. In answer to their question, "What does it mean to be Christian?" they experienced a call to serve the poor in Rome. This service began very simply by helping poor children with their homework. The young people soon became friends with these children and their families and at the same time they themselves drew into a community. In 1973 the Vatican offered this growing community an

old Carmelite monastery no longer inhabited by cloistered nuns, San Egidio in Trastevere, which they transformed into a centre. . . . From ten students the San Egidio Community has grown to include tens of thousands of members in many countries in the world. These men and women live in their own homes and work to support themselves. Each member is committed to listening to the scriptures in common prayer and to working with the poor. Service to the victims of urban disintegration takes many forms and is done on a volunteer basis. . . .

San Egidio communities also work closely with local churches in the areas where they are present, like Santa Maria in Trastevere. . . . San Egidio reflects the servant model, reaching out to the poor in its very midst and reminding us that this commitment is at the heart of the gospel message. Discipleship includes feeding the hungry, clothing the naked, welcoming the stranger, and reconciling enemies. The community of San Egidio challenges us to ask: Where are the poor? Where are we?[6]

It is interesting to look at San Egidio because of the numerous similarities that exist between it and the L'Arche communities: gestation in the 1960s; exponential growth in subsequent decades; international outreach; prioritizing of the poor, wounded, and marginalized; focus on the laity. In fact, Vanier's occasional encounters with San Egidio bear testimony to their shared vision:

In September, the Community of San Egidio organized a big interreligious meeting in Lyon. I participated in a round-table discussion with a Muslim philosopher and a rabbi on "an anthropology for the twenty-first century." Very interesting! The vision of the human being evolves, is transformed and deepens throughout the centuries. The closing ceremony, with the kiss of peace between rabbis, imams, Muslim theologians and leaders of Christian churches—and the whole meeting itself—was a real witness to unity and peace.[7]

The ecumenical and interfaith dimensionality of both these singular and iconic ecclesial movements—L'Arche and San Egidio—bear ample witness to the call for meaningful action in a time of chaos, violence, religious discord, ethnic genocide, and environmental desecration.

Although both have been led by charismatic lay leaders—Jean Vanier and Andrea Riccardi respectively (in addition to being men of applied pastoral instinct they are academic philosophers by training)—L'Arche and San Egidio are not structures encased in stone. They adapt, they morph, and they evolve.

A decade later, Vanier was in Assisi for the tenth anniversary of John Paul II's international gathering of world faith leaders in the city of Francis and this particular commemoration was organized by San Egidio:

> We all came together to share and pray for peace and to be a sign of peace and of prayer today. There were various workshops where Muslim leaders, rabbis, bishops and other leaders met together and shared topics. I was part of the workshop on "the love of God and the love of people." I shared especially about Ghadir, a young Muslim girl with severe disabilities whom we had welcomed in our L'Arche community in Bethany, and how my encounter with her had been a sign of God and a place of transformation for me.[8]

The common path shared by San Egidio and L'Arche around interfaith issues—transcending doctrinal boundaries to serve others in compassion; finding universal mission in the quest for peace; electing a pastoral strategy of nonviolence when encountering personal and structural intransigence and hostility—continue to define these lay communities and the gentle and yet formidable charisma of the two founders.

If Vanier was drawn to the zeal, energy, focus, and discipline of the ecclesial movements that thrived during the pontificate of the Polish Pope, he, like Riccardi, maintained a progressive independence, deeper ecumenicity, broader spiritual openness, and more flexible ecclesiology than is found in most of these movements. The spirit of the 1960s, the legacy of the Second Vatican Council, and the theological horizons that arose out of a time of creative and spiritual fecundity, defined their approach to leadership and mission. It is no surprise that there are congruences and confluences aplenty.

If Vanier had only occasional moments of connectedness with other like bodies or with parallel institutes, personal prelatures, and ecclesial movements, he did have a long and productive relationship with the pope himself. In August 1998 Vanier noted approvingly:

> John Paul II invited me and three other founders of new lay communities to speak to a gathering at which he presided, of some 350,000 people who have made a commitment within these new communities. I was asked to speak about the vision and spirituality of L'Arche and Faith and Light. Pascal Denardo, a Core member of Le Val Fleuri, was with me. During the Sunday Mass celebrated by the Pope, he brought the offerings to the Pope, who embraced him. . . . When I am invited to speak at such events, I know that it is in the name of each one of us at L'Arche. I know that I am just a voice, a bit like John the Baptist, the voice which points to Jesus, hidden in the weak, and to the power they have to transform us if we welcome them with compassion and truth.[9]

Often when Vanier traveled in order to speak about the work of L'Arche, he would bring an associate or core member. He did this because it provided him with precisely the opportunity to recede while others took the stage. It was a Baptist moment: "I know that I am just a voice, a bit like John the Baptist, the voice that points to Jesus, hidden in the weak, and to the power they have to transform us if we welcome them with compassion and truth."[10]

In the same way, Vanier saw John Paul II as a voice, summoning the religious world to a new and greater understanding, and in this, the pope was genuinely prophetic. The Assisi gathering—the first interreligious meeting initiated by the Polish pontiff—was "a radical movement, [an] incredible, audacious innovation" that brought everyone together in a way that one couldn't imagine. Like John the Baptist, John Paul II called out from the wilderness of our disunity, served as herald for a new path toward concord and harmony, and did this *not* in Rome but in Assisi, the small Umbrian walled city that embodies still the spirit of its greatest son: Francesco Bernardone.

Although Vanier has remained steadfastly reluctant to be drawn into the debates, controversies, and squabbles of competing ecclesiological paradigms; the cut and thrust as well as negativity that define ecclesiastical politics; and the fierce battles around the style and legacy of Karol Wojtyla, he is not unaware of them. His own more closely honed appreciation of the renewal and reform generated by the Second Vatican Council, his indifference to matters of clerical governance and conformity, and his evangelical priorities meant that his relationship with the pope was spiritual, not juridical, driven more by their shared commitment to spiritual empowerment as opposed to theological dissent, discipline, and delation.

A year before John Paul II died, Vanier found himself in Rome at the invitation of the Congregation for the Doctrine of the Faith, run by the Prefect Joseph Ratzinger and the man soon to be elected as Benedict XVI. It was an invitation that had special appeal for him: to attend an international symposium on the dignity and the rights of people who were mentally disabled. As biographer Kathryn Spink rightly notes, John Paul's own message to the symposium would have been especially inspiring for Vanier. The sentiments and convictions expressed by the pope echo Vanier. It is hard to imagine that his own writing and witness were not operative in the pope's mind as he penned his words:

> There is no doubt that in revealing the fundamental frailty of the human condition, the disabled person becomes an expression of the tragedy of pain. In this world of ours that approves hedonism and is charmed by ephemeral and deceptive beauty, the difficulties of the disabled are often perceived as a shame or a provocation and their problems as burdens to be removed or resolved as quickly as possible. Disabled people are, instead, living icons of the Crucified Son. They reveal the mysterious beauty of the One who emptied himself for our sake and made himself obedient unto death. They show us, over and above all appearances, that the ultimate foundation of human existence is Jesus Christ. It is said, justifiably so, that disabled people are humanity's privileged witnesses. They can teach everyone about the love that saves us; they can become heralds of a new world, no longer dominated by force, violence and aggression, but by love, solidarity and acceptance, a new world transfigured by the light of Christ, the Son of God who became incarnate, who was crucified and rose for us.[11]

The phrases "living icons of the Crucified Son" and "humanity's privileged witnesses" are classic L'Arche and speak eloquently to John Paul II's special relationship with people who are disabled, a relationship that enhanced his appeal to Vanier.

But perhaps the most telling and moving encounter between these two spirits would come shortly after the symposium at the shrine of Our Lady of Lourdes in France. On this occasion—August of 2004—Vanier, who had been invited to join the pope's personal pilgrimage to Lourdes, found himself walking beside the popemobile and recognized by this proximity how seriously disabled the pope had become. Parkinson's disease had ravaged the pope; he could barely communicate. Still, the pope could see that Vanier himself was feeling burdened by the heat and summoned him over in order to pat him on the cheek and give him his private rosary. It was an act of holy solidarity; it was a moment, as Spink says, of "extraordinary communion."

When Wojtyla died Vanier was deeply moved:

> The death of John Paul II affected me more than I expected. I knew and loved him personally and felt that he understood, loved and supported L'Arche and Faith and Light. . . . John Paul II was extraordinary in the way he called people in his church to be both rooted and open. We are called to be rooted in our faith, in the Gospel, in our particular church, and at the same time open to other churches, other religious traditions, other men and women of goodwill, discovering and appreciating the gifts of each one.[12]

If the leadership of Karol Wojtyla is defined by his often autocratic insistence on obedience, his hostility to and contest with anti-Christian ideologies sometimes to the detriment of detente and diplomatic compromise, and his wagging finger of disapproval (the infamous reprimand of Father

Ernesto Cardenal of Nicaragua comes to mind), a visual reminder of his disdain for dissent, then it is hard to fathom Vanier's undoubted admiration and love for the man.

But if the leadership is defined rather by the pope's passionate advocacy for a culture of life over a culture of death, by his personal heroism in defying architects of doom and engineers of dictatorship, and by his unstinting identification with, and visceral empathy for, the weak and suffering, then Vanier's view is both credible and laudable.

Quite simply, Vanier loved Pope St. John Paul II. As Pope Francis biographer Austen Ivereigh observes, "John Paul II needed converting [to the realization that the disabled are a living and constant reminder to the world of the supremacy of the heart]. . . . At breakfast with the (then fit and healthy) Pope in 1987, Vanier found that John Paul II had difficulty understanding what he meant by a disabled person having a healing presence. Then the Pope got sick, and 'a deep bond arose between us. . . . Our Pope is poor. He is fragile, but he is the glory of God.'"[13]

If his friendship with a pope was so rewarding and generative of good things, Vanier's friendship with one of the leading spiritual writers of his time—the psychologist-priest Henri J. M. Nouwen—would prove to be spiritually fecund beyond both their imaginings.

CHAPTER SEVEN

The Marriage
of Heaven and Hell

Vanier and Nouwen

The friendship of Jean Vanier and Henri Nouwen is one of the more dramatic, iconic, and deliciously complex spiritual relationships of the twentieth century.

It all began with Nouwen mentioning Vanier and L'Arche in his 1979 book *Clowning in Rome: Reflections on Solitude, Celibacy, Prayer, and Contemplation:*

> Personally I have found enormous strength in the witness of the Taizé community although I have never been there. I have found great hope in the work of Jean Vanier although I have never met him. I have found much comfort in just knowing about the work and life of the Little Brothers and Little Sisters, the Missionaries of Charity, and the San Egidio Community. These communal ministries give hope to our world and prevent us from joining the many pessimistic voices which de-energize us.[1]

Vanier was intrigued. He asked Jan Risse, founder of the L'Arche community in Mobile, Alabama, to contact Nouwen, and she invited him to a silent Covenant Retreat in Chicago that two L'Arche-related Jesuits, Bill Clark and Larry Gillick, were directing. That guaranteed their first meeting.

From the outset, they discovered kindred spirits. They talked before and after breakfast and at every opportunity they could find. They shared much in common despite their clear differences of style, personality, and background.

But it was their next meeting that proved determinative. Teaching at Harvard Divinity School, Nouwen invited Vanier to speak to one of his classes. What Vanier discovered was revealing: Nouwen was deeply appreciated and loved by his students, and he was in so many ways an amazing success, but he was also dissatisfied with his life as a professor, disconnected from his pastoral ministry, and adrift in the academy.

An immediate, if only partial, remedy suggested itself.

Come to L'Arche. Vanier addressed Nouwen's anxiety and fear around coming to L'Arche by observing to him that "maybe our people could offer you a *home*."

Nouwen accepted. He signed off on several decades of teaching (Notre Dame, Yale, and Harvard) and moved into a new orbit, one that would have him spinning for years to come.

Vanier recognized from the outset that Nouwen was a person who had the power to attract people with the affectivity and the intelligence of a charismatic. Nouwen's commitment to the people of South America impressed Vanier enormously, and he sensed that his presence at L'Arche would not only assist the community in its own mission but also introduce what they do to the people in the United States. Vanier reasoned that there were no important theologians who knew L'Arche at this point in its history, and that it could only benefit from having Nouwen associated with it.

In turn, Nouwen discovered from meeting the elders at the Covenant Retreat in Chicago that L'Arche was a place of relationship, a place where he could ply his trade as a spiritual writer, help people come closer to Jesus, and achieve the kind of human bonding that was absent at Harvard.

Vanier understood Nouwen's desperate yearning for relationships, his desire to go deeper into his friendships. He was aching for permanency. And Vanier understood that when Nouwen accepted his invitation to come to Trosly, he was accepting the privilege and the burden of being a mentor for him. Vanier knew that Nouwen was looking for community, that he saw in L'Arche a vision for the church of the future, but at the core of his accepting the invitation was Nouwen's awareness that he would have the chance to get to know Vanier better. He would have the grace of proximity.

This was going to be a problem. Vanier's numerous commitments, travel obligations, and high regard for personal boundaries and privacy meant that he was not going to be the steady and constant presence Nouwen required or expected. Also, the general untidiness and gentle pandemonium of L'Arche was a world apart, a world foreign to Nouwen, who was accustomed to Ivy League conventions and luxuries.

Life at Trosly was full of the disorderly; mealtime, except in Madame Vanier's quarters, was complicated and messy. The transition for Nouwen was a huge challenge. Vanier recalled in conversation with CBC radio producer Kevin Burns:

> He lived with Pauline, my mother, and at first it was as painful for her as it was for Henri. There were a lot of things he just didn't realize, like taking the cheese he saw out of the fridge and eating it. But it was my mother's cheese and he didn't ask her beforehand. A little *frisson* for sure.

> Still, they got around it. They would have long conversations, he would say Mass in her rooms, and she loved him

very deeply. She was instrumental in getting him to write a book about the Sacred Heart, her favourite devotion. Although he took the book in a slightly different direction than originally envisioned—it was published in 1989 as *Heart Speaks to Heart: Three Gospel Meditations on Jesus*—he remained faithful to my mother's injunction to let the heart of Jesus touch his own heart.

He bonded beautifully with her; but with me there were difficulties. He was frustrated that I wasn't always there for him, that I had to make time for a visit with him, that I was simply not available for him whenever the need arose for a chat, a walk, a probe, assistance in discernment. Anything, really.

I think maybe in some ways I was a disappointment for him and I can understand that. He was somebody *craving* for relationships.

It was clear that Nouwen's time at Harvard had been far less satisfying for him than he thought would be the case. Not that he didn't form wonderful friendships, influence students, make important pastoral contacts, and find new areas of interest to explore, only that a combination of factors—personal and professional—contributed to growing unease and mounting unhappiness. Trosly offered a way out; it offered him an antidote to the Harvard disease—obsession with intellectual accomplishment, the art of the mind, not the heart. Nouwen outlines the difference in a diary entry he makes during a retreat:

One of the most important things that Jean Vanier is saying to me during this retreat is that L'Arche is built upon the body and not upon the word. This helps to explain my struggle in coming to L'Arche. Until now my whole life has been centered around the word: learning, teaching, reading, writing, speaking. A good day is a day with a good conversation, a good lecture given or heard, a good book read, or a good article written. Most of my joys and pains are connected with words.

L'Arche, however, is built not on words, but on the body. The community of L'Arche is a community formed around the wounded bodies of handicapped people. Feeding, cleaning, touching, holding—this is what builds community. Words are secondary. Most handicapped people have few words to speak, and many do not speak at all. It is the language of the body that counts most. . . . Somehow I have come to think about eating, drinking, washing, and dressing as so many necessary preconditions for reading, speaking, teaching, or writing. Somehow the pure word was the real thing for me. Time spent with "material" things was necessary but needed to be kept to a minimum. *But* at L'Arche, that is where all the attention goes. At L'Arche the body is the place where the word is met. It is in relationship to the wounded body of the handicapped person that I must learn to discover God.[2]

Clearly, Nouwen learned much from his experience at Trosly. Although he would write about his experience at the epicenter of the L'Arche world, Vanier remembers him less as a theologian, writer, or spiritual thinker and more as a very lonely man yearning to meet people, having conversations, and resting. He was an exhausted person desperately in need of the curative, the healing powers, of a deep rest, unhampered by pressing obligations, schedules, publication deadlines, and emotional trials.

Nouwen's time with Vanier was a breakthrough time. From Trosly, Nouwen would go to Daybreak, the major North American L'Arche home in the greater Toronto area, and that would begin an association that would last a decade up to and including his death in 1996.

Vanier's Daybreak colleagues negotiated the agreement that would bring Nouwen to Canada's premier L'Arche home, and they knew that this would require a trial period, some adjustment, and that it wouldn't be an easy transition. After all, if Trosly was a respite, a sanctuary, and retreat, Daybreak was going to be a clearly delineated working as well as living relationship/contract.

Vanier saw Nouwen's coming to Daybreak as an immense gift for the community. His theological capacity, popularity as a writer of spiritual books, and his reputation as a preacher of renown meant only good things for the Daybreak profile, in particular, and for the L'Arche profile, in general. The Daybreak expectation that Nouwen would be an ideal pastor would soon be confirmed.

Vanier's judgment that Nouwen would make Daybreak known was vindicated in many ways, but especially in his book about his friend Adam Arnett, a man who was severely disabled, who could not speak or move without assistance, suffered from seizures, and whose death Nouwen chronicled in his moving memoir *Adam: God's Beloved,* finished just a few months before his own death in Holland:

> Adam's life and our relationship have been such true and lasting gifts for me. From a worldly perspective telling about our relationship makes no sense at all. But I, Henri, Adam's friend, decided to write it down. I didn't embellish it. I didn't soften or sweeten it. I tried to write it as simply and directly as I could. I am a witness of Adam's truth. I know that I couldn't have told Adam's story if I hadn't at first known Jesus' story. Jesus' story gave me eyes to see and ears to hear the story of Adam's life and death. It was in the light of that story that I felt compelled to write about Adam's story as simply and directly as I could.

L'Arche became my community and Daybreak my home
because of Adam—because of holding Adam in my arms
and touching him in complete purity and complete freedom.
Adam gave me a sense of belonging. He rooted me in the
truth of my physical being, anchored me in my community,
and gave me a deep experience of God's presence in our life
together. Without having touched Adam, I don't know where
I would be today. Those fourteen months at Daybreak,
washing, feeding, and just sitting with Adam, gave me the
home I had been yearning for; not just a home with good
people but a home in my own body, in the body of my community, in the body of the church, yes, in the body of God.[3]

Vanier was convinced that Nouwen needed a place of
grounding, a home where he knew he was loved and could
love. That home was Daybreak. In this L'Arche establishment he would find a home where he could form relationships, meet people, develop as a human being, not as a
celebrity, but as Adam's friend. Ever astute to the advantages
of meaningful and productive collaborations, Vanier could
see that what was good for Nouwen was good for Daybreak
and therefore L'Arche International.

Nouwen's arrival at Daybreak served Vanier's purposes
on several fronts. He brought his gifts for liturgy, spiritual
uplift, and friendship to the community, and he deepened
its familial maturity. As Vanier noted, Nouwen's theatricality, his love of spectacle, his animated Eucharistic celebra-
tions—wild gesticulations, pacing up and down, lively
preaching—enriched the prayer life of the Daybreak folk
but also allowed them the freedom to crave a true union
with Jesus. But as always, Vanier tempered his praise with
awareness of the larger truth—Nouwen brought his desires
into alignment with the community's, his need for relationship, his need for affirmation, and his need for fidelity.

This, of course, spoke to Vanier's own concern for creating life-giving, life-sustaining collectives—not constructs of ideological intention, political cells strategizing revolution, or kibbutzim united for a common end—but genuine communities that modeled a new way of being human. As he told Kevin Burns:

> Nouwen was deeply Catholic in the sense that he was deeply universal. He had a message, like a missionary. His message proffered a new vision for the world, a message of love, fidelity and friendship that could not be suborned by political propaganda or platforms.
>
> In fact, his spirituality was more rooted in human experience than it was in the scriptures. His understanding of the word of God, of the Gospels, was experiential more than theological. He was interested in beginning with his own humanity, which he explored and dissected with a searing honesty, and from that foundation drew universal conclusions. People responded to him because they *read* themselves in his writing and in his public appearances.
>
> In his own anguished search for body-soul unity, his desire to bring materiality and spirituality together, to end the false dualisms that haunt Christianity, people could see their struggles in his.
>
> This struggle for unity was primarily psychological but not exclusively. It had a strong justice component. He made the pain of South America his pain and he was a liberationist without ever subscribing to a theological school, academic hermeneutic, or political party. There was nothing Marxist, Hegelian, or Communist about his thinking but he was craving, yearning for unity, a unity that was in no way conformist, statist, or authoritarian.

Nouwen was terribly interested in the world and in everything that was going on around him. He was endlessly curious. The painful, the beautiful, the tortured, and the holy: it was all grist for his spiritual mill. He deplored the polarizations that define our time in both society and in the church.

He was thrilled by everything that is human: art, poetry, the circus, people in the throes of dying, infants being born—everything and everyone. There was something incarnational about him; he wanted to see things enfleshed. He ached for unity.

Aware of Nouwen's many gifts, Vanier sought to magnify their effect for L'Arche, but he also knew that the Dutch priest-psychologist, spiritual celebrity, and renowned retreat-giver and preacher was needy, dependent emotionally on others, and adrift and that L'Arche could be his port in a storm.

A brilliant calculation that could see all parties benefit from a rich reciprocity.

One of the things that appealed to Vanier was Nouwen's quest for unity. That quest, personalized, particularized, and subject to public scrutiny by Nouwen in his writings, was the quest of L'Arche as well and constitutive of its very vision. In that sense, Vanier's view of the unity that all of creation is aspiring to—a view that is biblical and Teilhardian, a view that is fully ecumenical in its realization—is a unity that transcends the policies and programs of state and the philosophical and pragmatic paradigms that define how nations and cultures see themselves.

In this way, Vanier sees Nouwen as part of a movement, a universal searching for unity, which is continuous, comprehensive, and extraterritorial. It is a searching that is open to experience, interprets that experience through the heart, weighs it through recollected wisdom, and tests it through discernment. Nouwen, in Vanier's view, was open in that searching, never despaired of the process of becoming, and was fecund in thought and feeling. The very term *fecundity*—a term Nouwen used regularly—had special appeal to Vanier, as he clarified in his Burns interview: "Nouwen was fond of the term and used it often. I think I first heard it in our conversation around the notion of communion. It could have been at a meeting in South Bend, Indiana. Wherever, it exemplified Henri's own fertility of feeling and thought: ever moving ahead, reflecting, deepening, being."

The most extensive treatment Nouwen gave the term was in his work *Lifesigns: Intimacy, Fecundity, and Ecstasy in Christian Perspective*, a work whose gestation originated in Trosly, a work whose central themes were provided by Vanier himself. In fact, Nouwen dedicated the book to both Vaniers—Pauline and Jean. In it, he speaks eloquently of what he understands fecundity to mean:

> "Those who remain in me, with me in them, bear fruit in plenty" (John 15:5). With these words Jesus speaks about fruitfulness or fecundity. When Jesus and all humanity through him have become our true home, we can become truly fecund or fruitful people. The word "fecundity" is not used often in daily conversation, but it is a word worth reclaiming, for it can put us in touch with our deepest human potential to bring forth life. That the word fecundity sounds archaic may indicate the reality to which this word points is receding to the background of our consciousness in today's technological society. . . . Fecundity brings forth life. God is a God of the living, and wherever God's loving presence becomes known, we see life bursting forth. Both sterility and productivity carry the seeds of

death within them. Fecundity always means new life, life
that manifests itself in new, fresh, and unique ways: a child,
a poem, a song, a kind word, a gentle embrace, a caring
hand, or a new communion among the nations.[4]

For Nouwen, Trosly meant the bringing forth of new life
in sharp contrast to the aridity, monotony, aggressive emotional disengagement, and frightful competitive ruthlessness
of Harvard. L'Arche offered the only sane antidote to the
maniacal ambition and work ethic of the Ivys, the only way
of ensuring that one's humanity is not sundered by success.
Vanier's community offered Nouwen not so much an escape
from the frantic energy and achievement-focused qualities
of Harvard, but a corrective, a redoubt, a sanctuary, and a
place where he could heal, become whole, and find a home.
In Vanier's view:

> Nouwen became very important to L'Arche. First of all, he
> understood it, as he showed especially in the book *Adam:
> God's Beloved*. Also, he had what I call the sacrament of
> the word. He knew how to say things that people would
> listen to and had a power of the word, especially the writ-
> ten word. And third, he was extremely authentic. He would
> have lost himself if he stayed at Harvard or Yale, but he
> found himself in L'Arche. He helped people to find them-
> selves, to discover a vision. You can see that this vision
> continues to touch me and flows through my letters even
> after his death in 1996.

Vanier's insight that Nouwen would flourish at L'Arche
and languish at Harvard was prescient. Many benefited from
his association—a fecund association—and few have man-
aged to condense that decade-long association with finer
equanimity and fairness than Carolyn Whitney-Brown, an
Elizabethan scholar with an Ivy League doctorate who

worked closely for years with Vanier and Nouwen. In an interview conducted for the CBC *Ideas* series on Nouwen, Whitney-Brown recalled:

> After Henri had been at Daybreak for ten years, there was going to be a discernment process, a process of working with Henri to determine whether the last ten years had been a good fit, whether the way in which he lived in community was healthy, good for him, good for the community, and how the next ten years would look.
>
> So, Daybreak invited two priests and Jean Vanier to come and participate in the discernment process and talk with the community. And so they spent a week touring around and talking to the Daybreak folk about Henri. The whole community was a hotbed of Henri stories with people discussing Henri and thinking about him.
>
> My husband, Geoffrey, and I met with Jean Vanier on the last day of the discernment. We talked frankly about Henri and the struggles he had with the community. People warped their lives out of shape so he wouldn't feel disappointed. But the gifts he brought were extraordinary: his gifts of joy, celebration and energy. He brought the outside world to our sometimes insular society. And the laughter.
>
> Throughout the week-long process as people told their Henri stories the laughter was unbelievable. Because he was so eccentric, quirky really, Vanier decided that we should do some skits as the finale of the discernment week: "Henri brings mirth to our community, which is really important, and we should revel in it at the conclusion of the process."
>
> Vanier was right. It became a carnival of delights. And we had so many distinguished guests and dignitaries—senior

leaders of the Catholic, Anglican and United Churches amongst many others—who were there for the skits. Vanier's idea to send up Nouwen in a proper L'Arche style was a bit startling and bold at first but confirmed his wisdom in reading character and the moment. Burst the bubble of solemnity with generous-hearted mockery.

For instance, there was a skit with Nouwen and his secretary with him having a nervous breakdown and her recommending that he read *his* books; a skit with Nouwen running around frantically, flinging his arms about while sermonizing, the hem of his cassock on fire while people are scurrying about removing candles; a parody of a Nouwen homily with handfuls of humus sprayed throughout the room celebrating our HUmanity and the HUmus of the world.

And so at the end of the evening we had sent up Nouwen in all sorts of ways: life in the community; Nouwen's anxieties; the stress he caused the community; the amusement; his travels; his teaching and lecturing; his spiritual leadership. All of it and we had done a really good job.

Vanier was pleased and so was Nouwen. Everyone laughed and heartily. Even the dignitaries forgot they were dignified and let their hair down. But the pièce de résistance came at the end of the evening after we had gathered all the cloths and candles and we were standing outside under the stars and loading everything into Henri's car to drive the short distance back to the Daybreak chapel where they were stored, when he stopped, looked at us with marvel and said, "I didn't think you knew me so well!"

Of course everybody knew him well. It wasn't possible to live with him and not know him well. But it was Vanier's brilliance to recognize that Henri wouldn't know that we loved him well if we just told him that; we had to *demonstrate* that we really knew him and loved him and wanted to love him and that his foibles and eccentricities were fine. We understood them better than Henri did and that they made him lovable to the community.

I think that in that moment he grasped how deeply he was loved. And this says as much about Vanier as it does Nouwen. Jean's wisdom was to know that through the skits, the laughter, the gentle fun, Henri would come to know, to feel, in his heart, in his gut, that L'Arche was his home.

No one could have anticipated that within a very short time after the discernment process Nouwen would die while traveling to St. Petersburg, Russia, to shoot a film documentary on his bestselling *The Return of the Prodigal Son*.

Daybreak prepared for his return from his aborted travels in a coffin. His "first funeral" was in the cathedral of Utrecht, with the principal presider Cardinal Archbishop and Primate Adrianus Simonis.

Vanier was the eulogist. He reminded the gathered of Nouwen's "prophetic vision," a term Nouwen himself defined as looking at people and this world through the *eyes* of God:

How are we going to live on without Henri? How are we going to be together as we feel the biting pain of his absence? Nobody can give answers to these questions but we must trust together we will discover new meaning among us. In fact, it is already happening. Henri's funeral has brought together people who are not comfortable in each other's presence. Healing and reconciliation are opening in the open space that Henri has left behind. The open space of a prophetic vision where we are not only Christians but others who are searching for truth, searching for love, searching for a real spirituality, a spirituality that will flow from the broken hearts of people, not through power but through the wounded hearts of people. So we must fill this empty space.[5]

Vanier's recognition that the heart of Nouwen's spirituality was inclusive and not dogmatic or restrictive, that his calling for a way of seeing others through the *eyes* of God was not formulaic or the special reserve of the religious but the common inheritance of all, meant that filling in the empty space left by his departure was going to be a universal summons.

Sue Mosteller, a Sister of St. Joseph, who for more than three decades served as an administrator, assistant, and housemate at Daybreak, has enjoyed deep friendships with both Jean Vanier and Henri Nouwen. The author of *Light through the Crack: Life after Loss*, Mosteller recounted for the CBC that one of the gifts Nouwen brought to L'Arche was not only a reawakening of the venerable tradition of befriending one's death, the spirituality of the *ars moriendi*, but the introduction to a way of burying that was tactile, sacramental, visceral, and holy:

> Our funerals at Daybreak were transformed because of his leadership. He taught us a lot about celebrating somebody's life. Every detail must be attended to. Celebrate the person in his entirety, allow the person to shine in our memory, weep, laugh, rejoice in the life of one who enriched our own and whom we loved deeply. Touch the body, embrace, kiss, talk—let the emotional and the physical have their place.

> This was the essence of everything he taught us. And so, when he returned—for his "second funeral"—we had this

marvelous celebration in the Slovak Catholic Cathedral of the Transfiguration in Markham, Ontario, where people came from far and wide. Well over a thousand people attended and the singing was over the top, exactly as Nouwen would want it. We wrote the intentions according to Henri's interest and we found the people to read them who best represented the constituency we had in mind. For example, Fred Rogers of PBS fame read the one about children, a mother read something about the family, representatives of the education field, advocates for those living with AIDS, and more besides participated. Some twenty-two petitions with a paragraph for each. This part of the liturgy alone gave ample proof of the breadth of this man's interests and loves.

The mood was festive, there was plenty of colour, sounds, smells, big flares of material cascading up the aisles, liturgical dancing, spirit movers who assisted the disabled as they too danced in their wheelchairs, spontaneous embracing, prolonged hugs, a Kiss of Peace that went on for a quarter of an hour, joy mixed with solemnity, grief displaced by hope. It was utterly theatrical, a spectacle of faith, a tangible sign of the body's worth, a liturgy of life.

Vanier knew what Nouwen could bring to L'Arche. And he knew that both Trosly and then Daybreak would give the itinerant professor, wandering priest, prolific writer, and anguished quester for Love's affirmation.

It was a fecund ten years.

CHAPTER EIGHT

The Humanist Philosopher

Mother Teresa was an activist; St. John Paul II, an ecclesiastical polymath; and Henri Nouwen, a psychologist-priest. Vanier's friendships with each of these people enriched him as a man and a thinker. The tendency to compartmentalize is common to us all, and the need to define by profession or career often supplants the higher calling—our vocation to be ourselves and to serve others.

Vanier succeeds in blending the pragmatic with the pastoral; he sees a problem, diagnoses it, recommends a strategy of repair or redress, and then acts upon it. He is the philosopher-activist *par excellence*.

The opportunity to deploy his training as a philosopher with his undoubted skill as a spiritual leader presented itself in the invitation to be the Massey Lecturer of 1998. The Massey Lectures—named after one of the governors general of Canada—is the prestigious five-hour lectures series prepared for and aired on CBC Radio's multi-award-winning intellectual affairs programs, *Ideas*. After the series is aired, it appears in book form and frequently generates a national discussion. Many of the most esteemed and storied savants of our time have given the lectures—academics, literary theorists, anthropologists, scientists, journalists, public intellectuals, historians, philosophers, theologians, poets, and novelists—and the published versions of the radio talks end up on university curricula around the world.

Vanier's choice—*Becoming Human*—was an instant success. Unprecedented numbers listened to the original airing, and the book was a national bestseller. Vanier had become a radio celebrity and a public figure in a way that was very different from the past. He was not speaking to or writing for an audience/readership of like-minded people. This was secular terrain. Big time.

He needed to find common ground, address listeners who might have an instinctively negative reaction to religious discourse of any kind, alight on themes and concerns endemic to all of humanity, transcend the limitations of tribal thinking, and do all of this at the same time, avoiding the pitfalls of magisterial utterance, oracular declamation, pious piffle, and the captivating shallowness of the sound bite.

The evidence is that he succeeded brilliantly. By being himself: part pastor, part thinker, fully human.

The opening lecture of the five-part series is titled "Loneliness," and in it he lays bare the foundation of his humanism:

> This book [series] is about the liberation of the human heart from the tentacles of chaos and loneliness, and from those fears that provoke us to exclude and reject others. It is a liberation that opens us up and leads us to the discovery of our common humanity. I want to show that this discovery is a journey from loneliness to a love that transforms, a love that grows in and through belonging, a belonging that can include as well as exclude. The discovery of our common humanity liberates us from self-centered compulsions and inner hurts; it is the discovery that

ultimately finds its fulfillment in forgiveness and in loving
those who are our enemies. It is the process of truly becoming human.[1]

The second lecture/chapter, "Belonging," addresses the
issue of Social Darwinism, the cult of the individual, the
tyranny of the collectivity as opposed to the community, the
power mystique of the successful class and the Superman of
Nietzsche. There is a beneficial and humanizing "belonging,"
and there is the kind that demands ideological conformity
and is defined by its rigidity and distrust of the individual.
Vanier reasons that without other human beings we self-
isolate, we withdraw into a cave of fear: "Our personalities
deepen and grow as we live in openness and respect, when
weakness is listened to and the weak are empowered, that
is to say, when people are helped to be truly themselves, to
own their lives and discover their capacity to give life to
others. Fear closes us down; love opens us up."[2]

The next lecture, "From Exclusion to Inclusion: A Path
of Healing," addresses the scandal that is Christianity. The
inversion of values represented by St. Paul, as understood
by Nietzsche in his *The Antichrist* and as embodied in in-
stitutionalized Christian truths that celebrate the weak over
the strong, the unlettered over the conventionally wise, the
powerless over the powerful, and that constitute the mad
contradiction, the mad paradox, of Mary's *Magnificat*, is
an inversion Vanier glories in:

> It seems paradoxical to say that people with disabilities
> have taught me what it means to be human and that they
> are leading me into a new vision of society, a more human
> society. With and through them I have discovered the joys
> of celebration, love, working, and communicating together
> in mutual respect and laughter. I realize more deeply how

spirituality flows from being human, or rather how spirituality is being fully human and so shapes our lives and our humanity. I have discovered the value of psychology and psychiatry, that their teachings can undo knots in us and permit life to flow again and aid us in becoming more truly human. I have myself experienced how religion can open us up to the universe, to the love of all humanity, and, especially, to the source of all life and love, to a meeting with God. This meeting with God, I find, is not first and foremost for those who are most clever and honourable but for those who are weak and humble and open to love, for those who take the way of the heart.[3]

The "way of the heart" is the way of L'Arche, of the radicality of Jesus' message and witness, of the "overthrow" of the safe orthodoxies, comfortable hierarchies, and established hegemonies that are the powers and principalities of our time, of any time, powers and principalities that can only be sundered by the simple, the innocent, the poor of spirit, the downtrodden, the forgotten.

The fourth lecture, "The Path to Freedom," underscores Vanier's conviction that it is imperative for the creation of a more deeply human society to find an antidote to our maniacally competitive culture. Quashing others—literally and metaphorically—in order to achieve, defining our worth by virtue of our success, scaling the ladder of promotion at all costs because our very identity is tied to it, all of these are symptomatic of our spiritual malaise. He asks:

Can we hope for a society whose metaphor is not a pyramid but a body, and where each of us is a vital part in the harmony and function of the whole?

I believe we can, because I believe that the aspiration for peace, communion, and universal love is greater and deeper in people than the need to win in the competition of life. But for this aspiration to become a real desire that inspires our activities, in order for it to break through our fears and the need to win, each one of us has to make a leap into trust: trust in the sacredness of every human heart, trust in the beauty of the universe, trust that in working for peace and unity, and in purging our false self, we will find a treasure.[4]

An authentic humanism is built on trust, relationships, intimacy, and vulnerability. It can only thrive when we address our common yearnings, recognize that outside of creeds, ideologies, and the plethora of intellectual and social constructs that make up our world, we are all called to the freedom God whispers in our soul.

In the final lecture, "Forgiveness," Vanier exhorts us to empower and free others—creating a new force of love and communion—by accepting Jesus' most daunting of challenges: to love our enemies. Such a love defies the logic of our experience, renders our world topsy-turvy, uproots our sense of tribe and social priorities, and calls us to a new and fuller humanity.

Vanier knows that L'Arche, his philosophy of being, and his theology of salvation are built upon the holy absurdity of Jesus' summons to new life in its fullness, a summons that runs counter to our instincts, our goals, and our sense of self. But it can be done. To demonstrate that forgiveness, love of one's enemies, is not a fantasy, a noble ideal perhaps but not realizable, Vanier draws on two distinct moments when the capacity for self-emptying love, the grace of an utterly gratuitous forgiveness, are historically concretized through the witness of two martyr-priests, Maximilian Kolbe and Christian de Chergé.

Kolbe, a Polish Franciscan, volunteered to replace a fellow inmate in Auschwitz who was condemned to be executed. The commandant of the camp was disarmed by the request but granted it, and Kolbe accompanied the other nine condemned men to the starvation bunker where he languished in acute pain until killed by lethal injection. Love conquered death, hope despair, self-oblation, and self-preservation.

De Chergé, Trappist abbot of a monastery in strife-ridden Algeria, was beheaded along with most of his community because they refused to abandon their witness to reconciliation and peace among their much-loved Muslim brothers and sisters. In a letter to his mother penned shortly before his demise, the abbot forgives his "friend of my final moment," his executioner, rising above hatred, self-pity, and resentment, divinizing the human through forgiveness.

Vanier celebrates the liberative, generative, and redemptive qualities associated with forgiveness near the very end of the series when he reflects:

> Forgiveness, the act of loving my enemy, like forgiveness of self, is not a sudden event, a rapid change of heart. Most of the time it is a long process that begins with the desire to be free, to accept ourselves as we are, and to grow in the love of those who are different and those who have hurt us as rivals. It is in the process of getting out of the prison of our likes and dislikes, our hatreds and fears, and walking to freedom and compassion. In the process of liberation, there may still be inhibitions, resentments, and anger, but there is also this growing desire to be free.
>
> I believe that this desire comes from God. . . .[5]

To be free, to trust, to accept our weaknesses and needs, to jettison the lust for competition—our unchecked entrepreneurial spirit—in favor of an equalitarian connectedness with all people irrespective class, education, social privilege, ethnicity, religious faith, or political allegiance is what it means to become human, and the true barometers of this new humanism can be found in the marginalized, the ignored, and the radically disabled.

This is *not* the wisdom of Athens, or Palo Alto, or Wall Street. It *is* the wisdom of the Broken One.

CHAPTER NINE

The Peacemaker

Pope John Paul II awarded Vanier the Paul VI International Prize for Peace and Development in 1997. It was apposite for a number of reasons, including a recognition associated with the Roman Pontiff who had traveled to the United Nations Assembly in New York City in the mid-1960s to declare solemnly and dramatically "war never again, never again war."

Vanier had long been an advocate for international peacemaking, as one would expect given his credentials as one striving through the L'Arche network to effect reconciliation and healing on the personal and familial levels, but perhaps a bit surprising given his military pedigree. Still, given the role played by his father, Georges, and Canadian diplomacy at large, around peacemaking missions, not surprising at all.

But Vanier received a jolt regarding the urgent need to make peace—like everyone else on the planet—on September 11, 2001. He noted in his introduction to his 2003 book, *Finding Peace,* "that the events of September 11 called me to become personally committed to peacemaking, to continue to reflect on peace and on the sources of violence in our world, in me, and in each one of us."[1]

For some time Vanier had been moved by the uncommon wisdom, passionate witness, and singular courage of the Dutch Jewish thinker, Etty Hillesum (*Etty Hillesum, An Interrupted Life: The Diaries, 1941–1943*). Murdered in Auschwitz she had observed that of the two torrents spreading over the world—"a torrent of loving kindness and a torrent of hatred"—she opted to struggle against hatred. Vanier was resolved to do likewise, to have her commitment reflected or continued in his own life. He valued Hillesum as one of the giant prophets of peace, and saw her as a model—"She wrote in her diary during the last year of her life: 'Ultimately, we have just one moral duty: to reclaim large areas of peace in ourselves, more and more peace, and to reflect it onwards to others. And the more peace there is in us, the more peace there will also be in our troubled world.' "[2]

"To reclaim large areas of peace in ourselves" is a project not only for those in straitened circumstances, poised on the precipice of extinction, persecuted and hounded, it is a project for all of us individually. Although it cannot be taken quantitatively as true, it is existentially so, that the more peace there is in our lives the more peace there will be in our world. So we must be peace-generators, our lives fruitful with peace, peace itself—with all its interior and external ramifications—our summum bonum as a society.

Peace among ethnicities, nations, and religions is graspable once we choose to operate our lives within an orbit of respect and trust. No one group is ontologically superior to another; no one group is privileged by birth and circumstance to lord it over others; no one group is treasured by God over others. There is no exceptionalism. We are all, *as persons,* loved into existence by God: "We can only be peacemakers if we believe that every person—whatever their culture, religion, values, abilities, or disabilities—is important and precious to God and if we seek to open our hearts to them."[3]

Every honest encounter with the Other provides us with an aperture onto the divine landscape of peace, unity, and harmony. Walls that separate us crumble in the face of our determination to speak out of our inner experiences, all "certitudes and ideologies" displaced by our inner silence.[4]

The perfect peacemakers are the ignored, the marginalized, and the vulnerable. Vanier provides an ideal example of what he means by this in a moving story drawn from India:

> One day we welcomed into our L'Arche home in Bangalore, India, a young lad with severe disabilities who had been living in the streets. He was hungry and covered in dirt. By the little hat he was wearing, we knew he was a Muslim. Cham, one of the men with disabilities who had been living in the home for quite some time and who was from a Brahman family, offered to share his room with this newcomer. Little by little, "Abdul,"—the name the community gave him, as he was unable to communicate his real name—opened up. He learned to walk and to do many of the same things as the other residents. One day an assistant accompanied him to a local mosque. Suddenly a voice cried out, "Elias!" It was "Abdul's" cousin. The lost boy had been found. A few days later a whole Muslim family arrived at our house. The elderly father told us, "My son is happy with you. He has made so much progress. We want him to stay with you." A friendship has grown between the L'Arche community and the family. And so sometimes it is the weakest ones, the least recognized, who can bring together people who are very different—not only in the community but also among neighbours, friends, and family—and set us on the path to peace.[5]

It is indeed the weakest, the most insignificant among us, who can "set us on the path to peace," for they are our, to use a phrase of Nouwen's, "barometers of the spirit." The answer to the crisis of 9/11, *the* crisis of our time, is an answer to be found only among the peacemakers, those who trust, those innocent of heart and not deadened to the humanity of others. How else do we respond to the explosive intolerance and mass murder conducted in the name of ruthless ideologies dressed up as religion? How else do we address the systemic evils that infect our political and social structures? Utopian? Madly optimistic? Unrealistic?

Perhaps. To the degree that the Gospel is unrealistic? The narrative and redemptive mystery of Jesus's life an exercise in grand fantasy?

For Vanier, the solution, the antidote, the answer is to be discovered not in political abstracts, enlightened manifestos, magnanimous global plans, or even inspiring leadership, although all these things are good and desirable, but in the essential humanness of us all, a humanness that Vanier sees beautifully realized in L'Arche, an emblem, an icon of sanity and sanctity:

> The strength of L'Arche is that its mission is deeply human. L'Arche is about helping people with a disability discover their human value, their personal beauty, and the importance of their own individual conscience. It is about helping them to see that behind their disabilities, their culture, and their human problems, lies their unique self. Some of our communities—such as those in India, Bangladesh, and Palestine—are made up of people of different religions, human beings who rejoice together and sometimes weep together. At the heart of L'Arche's life is the joy of communion.[6]

Increasingly preoccupied with creating a culture of peace in a strife-scarred planet, sensitive to the growing perception that religion is at the root of human discord, and keen on drawing the dialogue circle ever larger and larger, Vanier founded his pacific vision in the gospels. In a scintillating and reflective conversation with the ethicist Stanley Hauerwas, author of *Living Gently in a Violent World: The Prophetic Witness of Weakness* (2008), Vanier belaboured the obvious in an effort to highlight its importance:

> We have to come back to the gospel vision. . . . It is a vision of unity, peace and acceptance. It is a promise that the walls between people and between groups can fall, but this will not be accomplished by force. It will come through a change of heart—through transformation. It will begin at the bottom of the ladder of our societies. Jesus didn't spend too much time in the rich cities of Israel, such as Tiberias. He spent time with people who were caught in prostitution, the people they called "sinners" who were excluded from the temple. He spent time creating relationships. That's what Jesus did. His vision was to bring together all the children of God dispersed throughout the world. God cannot stand walls of fear and division. The vision of Jesus shows us that division is healed by dialogue and by meeting together.[7]

Dialogue, unity, mutuality, peace-creation—and all done from the base, the bottom of the ladder. The breaching of the walls, the erection of structures of respectful engagement, and the goodwill of religious leaders—these things can happen—but there is something more radical still that Vanier is calling for, something so radical that it puts him in exquisite congruence with Pope Francis:

> Jesus came to change a world in which those at the top have privilege, power, prestige and money while those at the bottom are seen as useless. Jesus came to create a body. Paul, in 1 Corinthians 12, compares the human body to

the body of Christ, and he says that those parts of the body that are the weakest and least presentable are indispensable to the body. In other words, people who are the weakest and least presentable are indispensable to the church. I have *never* [italics mine] seen this as the first line of a book on ecclesiology. Who really believes it? But this is the heart of faith, of what it *means* [italics mine] to be church. Do we really believe that the weakest, the least presentable, those we hide away—that they are indispensable? If that was our vision of the church it would change many things.[8]

Indeed it would. It would sunder the current model, overturn the ranks of entitlement, humble the powerful and the affluent, and drive Nietzsche mad. It would be an ecclesiology firmly set on the revolutionary impulses of the *Magnificat*. It would outdo Francis.

Hauerwas may not agree with Vanier's primitive ecclesiology—primitive in its pristine innocence and unsettling simplicity or literalness—but he has no difficulty seeing the L'Arche vision as essential for the church to be church. It "helps the church to find the gospel."[9] It is the canary in the mine.

Miners were accustomed to carrying canaries as a precaution against the insidious effects of the odorless and lethal methane gas found in their workplace. Once a canary perished they would know to flee the mine because of the presence of the deadly gas. L'Arche, Hauerwas concluded, is the church's canary: canaries bring us to the brink of a culture of death; they are the seeing sentinels in a dark place.

This is not an overly romanticized view of people who are disabled, a rationalization of their place in society that attaches a "special" significance to assuage our guilt. No, this is a recognition of the *humanizing* grace that they bring to all whom they encounter, the gift for reciprocity that allows one's vulnerabilities to be a means to growth.

Vanier sees in those who are disabled the stranger, the broken one, the very one that allows us to face our inside brokenness and to accept the fact that we are often strangers to ourselves. They force us to address our *own* brokenness as the necessary prelude to our entering into relationship with them, with those who are visibly, ostensibly, dependent and wounded.

In doing this, those who are disabled help us to "discern our natural inner protectiveness and compulsive attitudes. Somewhere we are hiding our weaknesses."[10]

The stripping away of the elaborately conceived shields that protect us from the truth of ourselves, a stripping that frees us up to see in our weaknesses our strength, is a stripping away of all that our natural and societal impulses recoil against. But in a society that wants to eliminate all "deficiencies," that sees all physical and emotional defects as expungable, that idolizes the perfect and successful at the expense of the imperfect and failed, the battle lines are firmly drawn.

Hauerwas plays the pragmatist to Vanier's optimist. He has a greater sense of realpolitik; he understands human pathology in a way that eludes Vanier. But not quite. Deploying military imagery, Hauerwas notes in his published conversation—*Living Gently in a Violent World*—that he is determined to be a warrior on L'Arche's behalf, that he is going to do battle with those forces aligned against the gentle communities of L'Arche, and that he can be counted on to be a fighter for the good.

But then he observes with sensitive astuteness that "where I see an enemy to be defeated, he sees a wound that needs to be healed. That's a deep difference."[11]

It is *that* difference that defines the Vanier vision. It is the *difference* that is the heart.

L'Arche provides a place where fear, emotional upheaval, ego needs, guilt, and shame can be negotiated. L'Arche provides a place where disagreement and discord can be softened by empathy and compassion. L'Arche can provide a place where communion can happen and bellicosity exorcized:

> Even moments of aggression between two people can find a place in this ample space of freedom and connection. Someone may be angry with another who touches something painful in his or her own history, but such tensions are tempered and made relative by the overall atmosphere of joyful shared emotions. A feeling of togetherness and of a common bonding seems to sum up this unique setting and its transforming encounters. We understand each other because relationships with ourselves and each other are at a good comfortable distance. There is no struggle to appear above the other or to be recognized.[12]

Because our highly stratified society is built on hierarchy, privilege, accomplishment, and ancestry, because our sense of our worth is measured, weighed, apportioned, and judged by quantifying assessments, and because we attach the highest importance to our independence, autonomy, and personal goal setting, the very idea that an alternative way of living is on offer, never mind infinitely superior in quality, is simply never entertained.

But such a way of living does exist and is a lifeline for those eager to know their deeper selves, eager to taste the interior freedom that comes with being liberated from the illusions, prevarications, and strategies of evasion that we put in place to protect us from our vulnerabilities.

Such a way of living is L'Arche.

Nathan Ball, a longtime L'Arche assistant, leader, director, and international coordinator, encapsulates the philosophy of L'Arche in a way that evokes its domesticity, native hospitality, and essentialist way of being:

A L'Arche community consists of a group of people who have decided to open one, two, three, five or more homes in which people with an intellectual disability and young caregivers or helpers live in a family-style way. These homes are typically in normal residential neighbourhoods and there are 146 such communities worldwide.

When you walk into a L'Arche house, you knock on the door, just as you would approaching any house. Someone will answer the door, welcome you generously in and if you were to stay for a few hours you would experience warm, every-day relationships between people with disabilities and the assistants. Cooking, cleaning, sharing their meals together; talking, laughing and negotiating conflicts. This is ordinary stuff.

The core of the L'Arche philosophy, the pedagogy upon which it is built, is the universal value, simple and unassailable, that every human being has not just a desire but a *need* to belong. Our response to the plight or the needs of people with disabilities is not to provide them with a service, or a stipend, or an employment program, as valuable as all these are, but first of all to say loudly and with deep conviction that we want to create *with* you a place of belonging because what turns out to be good and nurturing for the person with the disability is also good for those living and caring for that same person—in community, a shared enterprise, a body of healing.

The building up of the L'Arche communities, the universal oversight over their development and flourishing, and the active promotion of its credo occupied a great deal of Vanier's time even though throughout the first decade of the twenty-first century he was increasingly devolving more and more responsibilities unto the shoulders of his companions, indeed as he had gradually been doing since the early 1980s. Although his energy was largely sustainable, he needed to more carefully husband his time. He declined many honors and speaking occasions, traveled less and more discriminately, turned his attention to various writing enterprises that allowed him the chance to think more deeply upon things, and cherished his time at the home base: Trosly.

During the first two decades of the twenty-first century, serious, sustained, and soul-searching undertakings at the international level began both percolating and coalescing as a process of self-examination unfolded. Every living organism, every vital institution, must engage periodically in a substantive review of who they are, where they are going, and how they are going to get there. L'Arche is no different.

The mission and identity process—originating in 2002 at the general assembly at Swanick—culminated three years later with a new vision statement announced at the international federation meeting in Assisi in 2005. The questions they posed themselves were fundamental: What has our experience told us about the unique gift of L'Arche? What are the obstacles that prevent us from fully living L'Arche? What is the mission of L'Arche in the world today?

The new vision concentrated on three key words/concepts, and Vanier elaborated on their meaning in *An Ark for the Poor:*

> *Relationship* is an encounter or meeting, a gratuitous friendship, or a moment of communion between an assistant and a person living with a disability who has suffered rejection and humiliation. This is a relationship where each one receives and each one gives freely. The assistant discovers that he or she is not just to do good to people who have suffered from a disability, or to teach them, but to enter into a relationship of equality with them. This relationship is healing

both for the assistant and for people with a disability. It gives them each confidence in themselves as a person.

This relationship *transforms* not only people with disabilities but also the assistants. It gives the latter a new vision of society; it opens their hearts and spirits, helping them discover the sacredness of each person, whatever their culture, religion, capacities or incapacities. It implies a real humility, the capacity to listen and openness to the unexpected. It helps them each envision that the road to peace and justice in the world passes through these encounters that reveal the value and beauty of people too often hidden behind a disability, or behind a difference of culture, violence, depression or strange behaviour.

This transforming relationship becomes a *sign* of hope in our modern and highly technological world where there is rampant individualism, where mutual relationships are weakened, where each one has to be acclaimed and seen to be better than others, where rivalry and competition are encouraged, and where the weak are so often crushed. This relationship is a sign that things can change if we accept to enter into relationships of friendship with those who are weak and rejected.[13]

Relationship, transformation, sign: these three, as Vanier understands them, are critical determinants for effective ministry to people who are disabled. They describe the essentials for effective and mutual personal growth; they remind us—assistants, core members, and administrators—that the *Ark* is a place of creative reciprocity, spiritual maturation, a cocoon where freedom and trust shape us for a life of giving and receiving.

Throughout the decade, developments and alterations in the structure, governance, financing, and strategies of growth at L'Arche continued to occupy the attention of the community. General assemblies in Kolkata in 2008 and in Atlanta in 2012 continued to refine the mandate and philosophy, and Vanier exercised his role as *éminence grise*, the cofounder attentive to changes, accommodations, and new thinking with a serene attitude, nonproprietorial, detached, and disinterested. Vanier has been increasingly disengaged from the actual operations of L'Arche and in 2012 observed of his status and role:

> My role has been to live happily in my community. I repeat, "happily." I have wanted, by my life with people with a disability, to be a sign that it is a good and wonderful life in L'Arche and that people with disabilities are important in society and in the church and that they have gifts to give to all of us.

> L'Arche has an immense task in front of her to continue being a sign, I daresay especially in the churches. Up until now I had a voice in many church meetings. That was my grace and my mission [Vanier has spoken in countless Roman Catholic venues but has also addressed the Central Committee of the World Council of Churches in Geneva, the Lambeth Conference of the Anglican Communion, and numerous other ecumenical gatherings]. But my voice, because of my age, is becoming fainter. Because L'Arche is ecumenical, we do not belong to one particular church. The Roman Catholic Church can view us as a bit of an exceptional oddity. Other churches can see us as being too Roman Catholic.

> To whom do we really belong?[14]

In keeping with the original Vanier mission, people who are disabled belong to the world; they are a compassionate sign of God's mercy; they are a spiritual extraterritorial entity; they are a conduit of grace, a sign of *communio*.

Vanier's own discourse is redolent of Catholic analogies; as a Catholic philosopher he uses the tools and concepts that are familiar to him; as a Catholic religious thinker and spiritual leader he draws on the biblical narrative, the sacramental tradition, and the normative Christologies of the Roman Catholic Church. After all, it is his religious home. In *Befriending the Stranger* Vanier writes:

> In Trosly, after the community Eucharist on Holy Thursday, we all return to our homes where we wash one another's feet as Jesus asked us. Then we share a meal, the paschal lamb, and we tell our stories. Each one remembers what he/she has lived:
> "Where were you ten years ago?"
> "In a psychiatric hospital."
> "And you?"
> "I was alone, and very anguished."
> "And now we have been called together by God."
>
> We give thanks that we are no longer alone, that we have been called together, as brothers and sisters, a beloved people of God, walking together with God. That is the gift—and the miracle![15]

And this is the mystery that is L'Arche. Perhaps, precisely because of the personal nature of one's association—the relationship component—no better tribute to the L'Arche ministry and its efficacy and effectiveness can be found than in the record of people who have been at L'Arche as assistants. They know viscerally, existentially, the transforming power of this sign in their own lives.

James H. Clarke, lawyer, judge, writer, poet, father, and spouse chose with his artist-wife, Mary, to bring his young family with him to Trosly-Breuil for a nine-month period. It proved to be not a sabbatical but an epiphany. Out of his time at Trosly, Clarke would write his *L'Arche Journal: A Family's Experience in Jean Vanier's Community*, a human record charged with love. He later observed in an interview:

> I was about 36 at the time we moved to France. I had read about Jean Vanier's work and frankly I was looking for something different in my life. When I say "I," I mean my wife and kids as well. By this point in my life I had already achieved a fairly successful career as a lawyer. I enjoyed a very comfortable life in Coburg, Ontario, but I was searching for something else. I felt that in going to L'Arche and in opening myself to the experience of working with the intellectually disabled I would be stimulated and inspired by something new and different. I didn't really know anything about the world we were entering and I soon discovered that *indeed* I was entering a different world, a world that would upset many of my working assumptions and values.
>
> This whole new world was not the world I was accustomed to—the world of the talented, the powerful, and the successful. This new world was the world of the broken but open-hearted because the handicapped who confront you with their brokenness, and as a consequence introduce you to your own brokenness, do so precisely through their *lack* of intellectual sophistication, through their unnerving naturalness, their *lack* of artificial barriers erected by us to prevent real communion. They demand by virtue of their own generous giving a reciprocity that frees us; they create an environment that is very heartening.

Clarke, however, does not disguise the frustrations, failures, and foibles of community living; he has no time for "cheap grace." At one point in *L'Arche Journal* after marveling at Beauvais Cathedral "with its spaces of dazzling light," he pointedly observes: "Strange how dark, lifeless, and even forbidding the stained glass windows of the great cathedrals appear from the outside. But from the inside, what a contrast! Is this the experience of most people with the mentally challenged?"

Clarke quickly discovered that life with people who are challenged was indeed different viewed from the inside: it was incandescent rather than dark, a channel of hope rather than a cavern of despair. Many years after their experience at Trosly, the Clarke family would be deeply pained by Mary Clarke's suicide, a death by drowning that prompted the by then judge-poet and unforgetting lover to write "Proper Burial":

> O how we tried to give you a proper burial
> that sunny afternoon in Easter week,
> while your portrait gazed at us
> from the sanctuary,
> sprinkling you with holy water,
> robing you with incense,
> singing till we could no longer hear
> your unquiet spirit. And still
> at Eastertide I sometimes hear
> lilies weeping in the sun, your voice
> like Niagara, roaring in the night[16]

Who knows if the exquisite pain of such a loss—the haunting memories, the tortured cry of love, the obsessive "why"—could not in part have been mitigated by their earlier shared experience at L'Arche. Shortly before they left Trosly, Clarke noted in his journal:

> Before going to bed Mary and I had a long discussion. Our months at L'Arche have gone by so quickly! Not only have we witnessed the unique sufferings of the mentally challenged

but we have shared their special gifts of the heart: openness, sensitivity and capacity for moral and religious insight. . . . In a world where the massive rejection of the weak is commonplace, we believe L'Arche is an eloquent symbol of the equality and infinite value of all.[17]

For the Clarkes, as indeed for many thousands of assistants who have shared Vanier's vision for the wounded, the making whole of our fractured humanity is possible only when we attend to the logic of the heart. Vanier's *spirituality of the wounded* is a spirituality enmeshed in the world of broken bodies, broken minds, broken spirits. But Vanier knows to break open Albert Camus's "plague of cerebration" that poisons our culture, to expose to the open air the fallacies of reason, we must allow "the wounded" to heal *our wounds* and touch our invisible scars of heart and mind.

In short, we must be vulnerable as they are vulnerable. The "other" becomes a gift to us.

With the International Federation of l'Arche's adoption of its new identity and mission statement in 2008—a statement Vanier endorsed—L'Arche continues its metamorphosis, its unfolding, as a credible and enduring ministry for its time. The L'Arche that James Clarke knew is both the same and different from the L'Arche described by Hazel Bradley, the L'Arche Jubilee International coordinator:

A significant moment for the International Federation of L'Arche was the adoption of a new identity and mission statement which focused the communities' move away from solely offering homes and work to people with learning disabilities for life *to* being outward-facing communities of faith with mutual relationships and trust in God at the heart of our journey and responsive to changing needs and circumstances [italics mine].[18]

EPILOGUE

The Twilight Time

From 1981 when Vanier stepped down from the day-to-day responsibility for the original L'Arche community in Trosly and from the International Federation of L'Arche Communities in order to allow others to take over for him, Vanier has made every effort to implement the Catholic social principle of subsidiarity among those who work with him in the L'Arche network. By empowering others to assume leadership roles and stepping aside with the firm conviction that he is best an enabler and inspirer, Vanier modeled the kind of collegiality he sees at the heart of L'Arche governance.

Since 1981 Vanier has been able to concentrate on his writing, retreat giving, and lecturing through the present—the very year when he received the prestigious Templeton Prize.

With less energy, simply as a consequence of aging, and with astute spiritual prioritizing, Vanier in recent decades concentrated on publishing his thoughts and on bearing witness to peace in a parlous time (his personal intervention around the *Charlie Hebdo* massacre reminds us that he is no ideologue, laments the puerile arguments for freedom of speech that thrive on the denigration of others, and understands that only through peace and social concord can we secure the foundations of a genuine humanism).

This maturing of his thought is seen most clearly in his extended biblical reflection—*Drawn into the Mystery of Jesus through the Gospel of John*—an exercise in *lectio divina* that allowed Vanier to probe the deeper layers of Johannine wisdom precisely because he read the gospel not as an academic project with its rich conceptual structure but as a letter from a friend enfolded in the love of Jesus:

> The interpretation I have given of this Gospel of John
>   speaks of
> what is in my own heart,
> with my particular experience of faith, life and prayer
> rooted as well in what many wise and holy people
> of the past and present
> have taught by their words, their lives or their writings.
> In the Gospel of John,
> I have come to see that to pray is above all to dwell in Jesus
> and to let Jesus dwell in me.
> It is not first and foremost to *say prayers,*
> But to live in the *now* of the present moment,
> In communion with Jesus.
> Prayer is a place of rest and quiet.
> When we love someone, don't we delight in being with
>   each other,
> being present to one another?
> Now and again we may say a word of affection,
> we will be attentive to each other and listen to each other,
> but it is essentially a place of silence.
> The great Spanish mystic John of the Cross once said,
> "Silence is the way God speaks to us."

I learned the silence of prayer and the prayer of silence
with my spiritual father, Père Thomas Philippe.
He helped me to find silence in myself.
It is true that this silence is the fruit of the presence of God;
    it is peace.[1]

The young boy who learned the meaning of trust from
his father, the young man who was inspired by the suffering
of the abandoned, the struggling philosopher on a quest for
happiness, the spiritual writer yearning for the deepest communion, this man, now an esteemed elder, has come to taste
more fully the generative power of silence, the restorative
power of peace, and the liberative power of unrestricted
tenderness.

Trosly has never looked so good.

Notes

Chapter Two:
Père Thomas and Spiritual Friendship—pages 19–28

1. Kathryn Spink, *The Miracle, The Message, The Story: Jean Vanier and L'Arche* (Mahwah, NJ: HiddenSpring/Paulist, 2006), 45.

2. In his *Letter to the Duke of Norfolk* John Henry Cardinal Newman argued for the supreme authority of conscience, the law of God as "apprehended in the minds" of women and men, the very "aboriginal Vicar of Christ" in each one of us. Conscience for Newman was sovereign, as it was for Georges and Jean Vanier.

3. Jean Vanier, *Made for Happiness: Discovering the Meaning of Life with Aristotle* (Toronto: Anansi, 2001), 196–97.

Chapter Three:
L'Arche, the Beginning—pages 29–37

1. Kathryn Spink, *The Miracle, The Message, The Story: Jean Vanier and L'Arche* (Mahwah, NJ: HiddenSpring/Paulist, 2006), 63–64.

2. Jean Vanier, *Our Life Together: A Memoir in Letters* (Toronto: HarperCollins, 2007), 16–17.

3. Jean Vanier, *The Heart of L'Arche: A Spirituality for Every Day* (Toronto: Novalis, 2012), 28–29.

4. Ibid., 31.

5. Vanier, *Our Life Together*, 22.

6. Spink, *The Miracle, The Message, The Story*, 65.

Chapter Four:
A Death and an Inspiration—pages 38–45

1. Mary Frances Coady, *Georges and Pauline Vanier: Portrait of a Couple (*Montreal/Kingston: McGill-Queen's University Press, 2011), 249.

2. Jean Vanier, *In Weakness, Strength: The Spiritual Sources of Georges P. Vanier, 19th Governor-General of Canada* (Toronto: Griffin House, 1969), 20–21.

3. Ibid., 21–22.

4. Ibid., 37.

5. Jean Vanier, *Our Life Together: A Memoir in Letters* (Toronto: HarperCollins, 2007), 55.

6. Ibid., 118.

Chapter Five:
Growing Internationalism—pages 46–53

1. Jean Vanier, *Our Life Together: A Memoir in Letters* (Toronto: HarperCollins, 2007), 199.

2. Ibid., 207–08.

3. Ibid., 257–58.

4. Jean Vanier, *An Ark for the Poor: The Story of L'Arche* (Toronto: Novalis, 2012), 82–83.

Chapter Six:
Vanier and Wojtyla—pages 54–67

1. Jean Vanier, *Our Life Together: A Memoir in Letters* (Toronto: HarperCollins, 2007), 317.

2. Ibid., 319–20.

3. Michael W. Higgins and Douglas R. Letson, *Power and Peril: The Catholic Church at the Crossroads* (Toronto: HarperCollins, 2002), 304–05.

4. Higgins and Letson, *Power and Peril*, 315–16.

5. Vanier, *Our Life Together*, 21.

6. Ellen Leonard, "Emerging Communities of Dialogue and Mission," *Grail: An Ecumenical Journal,* vol. 8 (September 1992): 12–13, 23.

7. Vanier, *Our Life Together*, 530.

8. Ibid., 538.

9. Ibid., 444.

10. Ibid., 444.

11. Pope John Paul II, Message on the Occasion of the International Symposium on the Dignity and Rights of the Mentally Disabled Person (Rome: January 5, 2004).

12. Ibid., 525–26.

13. Austen Ivereigh, "Lessons from the Vulnerable," *The Tablet* (December 13, 2008): 22.

Chapter Seven:
The Marriage of Heaven and Hell—pages 68–83

1. Henri J. M. Nouwen, *Clowning in Rome: Reflections on Solitude, Celibacy, Prayer, and Contemplation* (New York: Image, 2000), 30.

2. Henri J. M. Nouwen, *The Road to Daybreak: A Spiritual Journey* (New York: Image, 1990), 150–51.

3. Henri J. M. Nouwen, *Adam: God's Beloved* (Maryknoll: Orbis, 2010), 126–27.

4. Henri J. M. Nouwen, *Lifesigns: Intimacy, Fecundity, and Ecstasy in Christian Perspective* (New York: Image, 1986), 43, 68.

5. Jean Vanier's eulogy for Henri Nouwen, September 25, 1996, as quoted in Michael W. Higgins and Kevin Burns, *Genius Born of Anguish: The Life and Legacy of Henri Nouwen* (Toronto: Novalis, 2012), 126.

Chapter Eight:
The Humanist Philosopher—pages 84–90

1. Jean Vanier, *Becoming Human* (Mahwah, NJ: Paulist, 2008), 5.

2. Ibid., 68.

3. Ibid., 97.

4. Ibid., 123.

5. Ibid., 161.

Chapter Nine: The Peacemaker—pages 91–106

1. Jean Vanier, *Finding Peace* (Toronto: Anansi, 2003), 4.

2. Jean Vanier, *Our Life Together: A Memoir in Letters* (Toronto: HarperCollins, 2007), 535.

3. Vanier, *Finding Peace,* 40.

4. Ibid.

5. Ibid., 65–66.

6. Jean Vanier, *Signs: Seven Words of Hope (*Toronto: Novalis, 2013), 65.

7. Stanley Hauerwas and Jean Vanier, *Living Gently in a Violent World: The Prophetic Witness of Weakness (*Downers Grove, IL: IVP Books, 2008), 29.

8. Ibid., 74.

9. Ibid., 57.

10. Ibid., 68.

11. Ibid., 80.

12. Vanier, *Signs,* 82–83.

13. Vanier, *An Ark for the Poor: The Story of L'Arche* (Toronto: Novalis, 2012), 117–18.

14. Ibid., 145.

15. Jean Vanier, *Befriending the Stranger* (Toronto: Novalis, 2009), 127–28.

16. Michael W. Higgins and Douglas R. Letson, *Power and Peril: The Catholic Church at the Crossroads* (Toronto: HarperCollins, 2002), 339–40.

17. Ibid., 340–41.

18. Hazel Bradley, "Networks of Friendship," *The Tablet* (March 14, 2015), 13.

Epilogue: The Twilight Time—pages 107–9

1. Jean Vanier, *Drawn into the Mystery of Jesus through the Gospel of John (*Toronto: Novalis, 2006), 358–59.

Bibliography

Primary Sources

Vanier, Jean. *In Weakness, Strength: The Spiritual Sources of Georges P. Vanier, 19th Governor-General of Canada.* Toronto: Griffin House, 1969.

———. *Tears of Silence.* Toronto: Griffin House, 1970.

———. *Eruption to Hope.* Toronto: Griffin House, 1971.

———. *Followers of Jesus.* Toronto: Griffin House, 1973.

———. *Be Not Afraid.* Toronto: Griffin House, 1975.

———. *Community and Growth: Our Pilgrimage Together.* Toronto: Griffin House, 1979.

———. *The Challenge of L'Arche.* Ottawa: Novalis, 1981.

———. *I Meet Jesus: He Tells Me "I Love You," Story of the Love of God through the Bible.* Mahwah, NJ: Paulist Press, 1981.

———. *I Walk with Jesus.* Mahwah, NJ: Paulist Press, 1985.

———. *Man and Woman He Made Them.* Mahwah, NJ: Paulist Press, 1985.

———. *Jesus, the Gift of Love.* London: Hodder & Stoughton, 1988.

———. *The Broken Body.* Mahwah, NJ: Paulist Press, 1988.

———. *Images of Love, Words of Hope.* Hantsport, NS: Lancelot Press, 1991.

———. *A Network of Friends, Volume One: 1964–1973, the Letters of Jean Vanier to the Friends and Communities of L'Arche.* Hantsport, NS: Lancelot Press, 1992.

———. *From Brokenness to Community.* New York: Paulist Press, 1992.

———. *An Ark for the Poor: The Story of L'Arche.* Ottawa: Novalis, 1995.

———. *The Heart of L'Arche: A Spirituality for Every Day.* Toronto: Novalis, 1995.

———. *The Scandal of Service: Jesus Washes Our Feet.* Ottawa: Novalis, 1996.

———. *Our Journey Home: Rediscovering a Common Humanity Beyond Our Differences.* Ottawa: Novalis, 1997.

Vanier, Jean, Anne-Sophie Andreu, and Michel Quoist. *A Door of Hope.* London: Hodder & Stoughton, 1996.

Vanier, Jean. *Becoming Human.* Toronto: House of Anansi Press, 2001.

———. *Made for Happiness: Discovering the Meaning of Life with Aristotle.* London: Darton, Longman & Todd, 2001.

———. *Seeing Beyond Depression.* London: SPCK, 2001.

———. *Finding Peace.* Toronto: House of Anansi Press, 2003.

———. *Drawn into the Mystery of Jesus through the Gospel of John.* New York: Paulist Press, 2004.

———. *Befriending the Stranger.* Toronto: Novalis, 2005.

———. *Our Life Together: A Memoir in Letters.* London: Darton, Longman & Todd, 2008.

Vanier, Jean, and Stanley Hauerwas. *Living Gently in a Violent World: The Prophetic Witness of Weakness.* Downers Grove, IL: IVP Books, 2008.

Vanier, Jean. *From Brokenness to Wholeness.* Singapore: Medio Media, 2012. CD.

———. *The Gospel of John, the Gospel of Relationship.* Cincinnati: Franciscan Media, 2015.

———. *Life's Great Questions.* Cincinnati: Franciscan Media, 2015.

Secondary Sources

Bradley, Hazel. "Networks of Friendship." *The Tablet* (March 14, 2015).

Coady, Mary Frances. *Georges and Pauline Vanier: Portrait of a Couple*. Montreal/Kingston: McGill-Queen's University Press, 2011.

Higgins, Michael W. *Henri Nouwen: A Spirituality for the Wounded*. Now You Know Media, 2013. CD.

———. "Henri Nouwen, Thomas Merton, and Donald Nicholl: Pilgrims of Wisdom and Peace." In *Turning the Wheel: Henri Nouwen and Our Search for God*, edited by Jonathan Bengtson and Gabrielle Earnshaw (Maryknoll: Orbis Books, 2007).

———. "In Weakness, Strength." *Literary Review of Canada* (May 2008).

———. "Messy Love: Jean Vanier's L'Arche." *Commonweal* (May 4, 2009).

———. "A Joy, Not a Nuisance: What the Disabled Taught Jean Vanier." *Commonweal* (December 18, 2015).

Higgins, Michael W., and Douglas R. Letson. *Power and Peril: The Catholic Church at the Crossroads*. Toronto: Harper-Collins, 2002.

Higgins, Michael W., and Kevin Burns. *Genius Born of Anguish: The Life and Legacy of Henri Nouwen*. Mahwah: Paulist Press, 2012.

Ivereigh, Austen. "Lessons from the Vulnerable." *The Tablet* (December 13, 2008).

Leonard, Ellen. "Emerging Communities of Dialogue and Mission." *Grail: An Ecumenical Journal* (September 1992).

Nouwen, Henri J. M. *Adam: God's Beloved*. Maryknoll: Orbis, 2010.

———. *Clowning in Rome: Reflections on Solitude, Celibacy, Prayer, and Contemplation*. New York: Image, 2000.

———. *Lifesigns: Intimacy, Fecundity, and Ecstasy in Christian Perspective*. New York: Image, 1986.

———. *The Road to Daybreak: A Spiritual Journey*. New York: Image, 1990.

Spink, Kathryn. *The Miracle, The Message, The Story: Jean Vanier and L'Arche*. Mahwah, NJ: HiddenSpring/Paulist, 2006.

Whitney-Brown, Carolyn. *Jean Vanier: Essential Writings*. Mary-
    knoll: Orbis, 2008.

Interviews

Vanier, Jean. Interview by Kevin Burns. Trosly-Breuil, May 2010.
Vanier, Jean. Interview by Eleanor Clitheroe, Michael W. Higgins,
    and Donald Morrison. Trosly-Breuil, September 2014.

Index